Marx Machiavelli Chesterton Emerson Joyce
Abbott Hardy Montaigne Cooper Austen
Defoe Melville Haggard Hugo
Christie Eliot Grimm
Stoker Carroll Molière
Wilde Maupassant Byron
Engels Schiller
Garnett Einstein Fitzgerald Smith
Goethe Hawthorne Kafka
Cotton Dostoyevsky Hall
Baum Kipling Doyle Willis
Leslie Dumas Henry Nietzsche
Flaubert Turgenev Balzac
Stockton Vatsyayana Crane
Burroughs Whitman Verne
Curtis Tocqueville Gogol Vinci
Homer Widger Tolstoy Busch
Darwin Thoreau
Potter Freud Zola Twain Plato Scott
Lawrence
Kant Jowett Stevenson Dickens
Andersen Burton Hesse Harte
London Descartes Cervantes
Poe Aristotle Wells Voltaire
Hale James Hastings Cooke
Bunner Shakespeare
Richter Chambers Irving
Chekhov da Shaw Wodehouse Benedict
Doré Swift Dante Alcott
Pushkin
Newton

tredition®

tredition was established in 2006 by Sandra Latusseck and Soenke Schulz. Based in Hamburg, Germany, tredition offers publishing solutions to authors and publishing houses, combined with worldwide distribution of printed and digital book content. tredition is uniquely positioned to enable authors and publishing houses to create books on their own terms and without conventional manufacturing risks.

For more information please visit: www.tredition.com

TREDITION CLASSICS

This book is part of the TREDITION CLASSICS series. The creators of this series are united by passion for literature and driven by the intention of making all public domain books available in printed format again - worldwide. Most TREDITION CLASSICS titles have been out of print and off the bookstore shelves for decades. At tredition we believe that a great book never goes out of style and that its value is eternal. Several mostly non-profit literature projects provide content to tredition. To support their good work, tredition donates a portion of the proceeds from each sold copy. As a reader of a TREDITION CLASSICS book, you support our mission to save many of the amazing works of world literature from oblivion. See all available books at www.tredition.com.

Project Gutenberg

The content for this book has been graciously provided by Project Gutenberg. Project Gutenberg is a non-profit organization founded by Michael Hart in 1971 at the University of Illinois. The mission of Project Gutenberg is simple: To encourage the creation and distribution of eBooks. Project Gutenberg is the first and largest collection of public domain eBooks.

The Religion of Numa And Other Essays on the Religion of Ancient Rome

Jesse Benedict Carter

Imprint

This book is part of TREDITION CLASSICS

Author: Jesse Benedict Carter
Cover design: Buchgut, Berlin – Germany

Publisher: tredition GmbH, Hamburg - Germany
ISBN: 978-3-8424-8638-6

www.tredition.com
www.tredition.de

The intention of the TREDITION CLASSICS series is to make world literature in the public domain available in printed format. Literary enthusiasts and organizations, such as Project Gutenberg, worldwide have scanned and digitally edited the original texts. tredition has subsequently formatted and redesigned the content into a modern reading layout. Therefore, we cannot guarantee the exact reproduction of the original format of a particular historic edition. Please also note that no modifications have been made to the spelling, therefore it may differ from the orthography used today.

TO

K.F.C.

PREFACE

This little book tries to tell the story of the religious life of the Romans from the time when their history begins for us until the close of the reign of Augustus. Each of its five essays deals with a distinct period and is in a sense complete in itself; but the dramatic development inherent in the whole forbids their separation save as acts or chapters. In spite of modern interest in the study of religion, Roman religion has been in general relegated to specialists in ancient history and classics. This is not surprising for Roman religion is not prepossessing in appearance, but though it is at first sight incomparably less attractive than Greek religion, it is, if properly understood, fully as interesting, nay, even more so. In Mr. W. Warde Fowler's *Roman Festivals* however the subject was presented in all its attractiveness, and if the present book shall serve [Pg viii] as a simple introduction to his larger work, its purpose will have been fulfilled.

No one can write of Roman religion without being almost inestimably indebted to Georg Wissowa whose *Religion und Cultus der Römer* is the best systematic presentation of the subject. It was the author's privilege to be Wissowa's pupil, and much that is in this book is directly owing to him, and even the ideas that are new, if there are any good ones, are only the bread which he cast upon the waters returning to him after many days.

The careful student of the history of the Romans cannot doubt the psychological reality of their religion, no matter what his personal metaphysics may be. It is the author's hope that these essays may have a human interest because he has tried to emphasise this reality and to present the Romans as men of like passions to ourselves, in spite of all differences of time and race.

Hearty thanks are due to Mr. W. Warde Fowler and to Mr. Albert W. Van Buren for their great kindness in reading the proofs; and the dedication of the book is at best a poor return for the help which my wife has given me.

J.B.C.
Rome, *November, 1905.*

CONTENTS

THE RELIGION OF NUMA

Rome forms no exception to the general rule that nations, like individuals, grow by contact with the outside world. In the middle of the five centuries of her republic came the Punic wars and the intimate association with Greece which made the last half of her history as a republic so different from the first half; and in the kingdom, which preceded the republic, there was a similar coming of foreign influence, which made the later kingdom with its semi-historical names of the Tarquins and Servius Tullius so different from the earlier kingdom with its altogether legendary Romulus, Numa, Tullus Hostilius and Ancus Martius. We have thus four distinct phases in the history of Roman society, and a corresponding phase of religion in each period; and if we add to this that new social structure which came into being by the reforms of Augustus at the beginning of the empire, together with the religious changes which accompanied it, we shall have the five periods which these five essays try to describe: the [Pg 2] period before the Tarquins, that is the "Religion of Numa"; the later kingdom, that is the "Reorganisation of Servius"; the first three centuries of the republic, that is the "Coming of the Sibyl"; the closing centuries of the republic, that is the "Decline of Faith"; and finally the early empire and the "Augustan Renaissance." Like all attempts to cut history into sections these divisions are more or less arbitrary, but their convenience sufficiently justifies their creation. They must be thought of however not as representing independent blocks, arbitrarily arranged in a certain consecutive order, not as five successive religious consciousnesses, but merely as marking the entrance of certain new ideas into the continuous religious consciousness of the Roman people. The history of each of these periods is simply the record of the change which new social conditions produced in that great barometer of society, the religious consciousness of the community. It is in the period of the old kingdom that our story begins.

At first sight it may seem a foolish thing to try to draw a picture of the religious condition of a time about the political history of which we know so little, and it is only right therefore that we should inquire what sources of knowledge we possess.

There was a time, not so very long ago, when under the banner of the new-born science of "Com [Pg 3] parative Philology" there gathered together a group of men who thought they held the key to prehistoric history, and that words themselves would tell the story where ancient monuments and literature were silent. It was a great and beautiful thought, and the science which encouraged it has taken its place as a useful and reputable member of the community of sciences, but its pretensions to the throne of the revealer of mysteries have been withdrawn by those who are its most ardent followers, and the "Indo-Germanic religion" which is brought into being is a pleasant thought for an idle hour rather than a foundation and starting-point for the study of ancient religion in general. Altogether aside from the fact that although primitive religion and nationality are in the main identical, language and nationality are by no means so—we have the great practical difficulty in the case of Greece and Rome that in the earliest period of which we have knowledge these two religions bear so little resemblance that we must either assert for the time of Indo-Germanic unity a religious development much more primitive than that which comparative philology has sketched, or we must suppose the presence of a strong decadent influence in Rome's case after the separation, which is equally difficult. If we realise that in a primitive religion the name of the god is usually the same as the name of the thing which he represents, the existence of a Greek god and a Roman god with names [Pg 4] which correspond to the same Indo-Germanic word proves linguistically that the *thing* existed and had a name before the separation, but not at all that the thing was deified or that the name was the name of a god at that time. We must therefore be content to begin our study of religion much more humbly and at a much later period.

In fact we cannot go back appreciably before the dawn of political history, but there are certain considerations which enable us at least to understand the phenomena of the dawn itself, those survivals in culture which loom up in the twilight and the understanding of which gives us a fair start in our historical development. For this knowledge we are indebted to the so-called "anthropological" method, which is based on the assumption that mankind is essentially uniform, and that this essential uniformity justifies us in drawing inferences about very ancient thought from the very primitive thought of the barbarous and savage peoples of our own day. At first sight the weakness of this contention is more apparent than its strength, and it is easy to show that the prehistoric primitive culture of a people destined to civilisation is one thing, and the retarded primitive culture of modern tribes stunted in their growth is quite another thing, so that, as has so often been said, the two bear a relation to each other not unlike that of a healthy young child to a full-grown idiot. And yet there is a decided resemblance [Pg 5] between the child and the idiot, and whether prehistoric or retarded, primitive culture shows everywhere strong likeness, and the method is productive of good if we confine our reasoning backwards to those things in savage life which the two kinds of primitive culture, the prehistoric and the retarded, have in common. To do this however we must have some knowledge of the prehistoric, and our modern retarded savage must be used merely to illumine certain things which we see only in half-light; he must never be employed as a lay-figure in sketching in those features of prehistoric life of which we are totally in ignorance. It is peculiarly useful to the student of Roman religion because he stands on the borderland and looking backwards sees just enough dark shapes looming up behind him to crave more light. For in many phases of early Roman religion there are present characteristics which go back to old manners of thought, and these manners of thought are not peculiar to the Romans but are found in many primitive peoples of our own day. The greatest contribution which anthropology has made to the study of early Roman religion is "animism."

Not much more than a quarter of a century ago the word "animism" began to be used to describe that particular phase of the psychological condition of primitive peoples by which they believe that a spirit (*anima*) resides in everything, material and immaterial. This spirit is generally closely associated [Pg 6] with the thing itself, sometimes actually identified with it. When it is thought of as distinct from the thing, it is supposed to have the form of the thing, to be in a word its "double." These doubles exercise an influence, often for evil, over the thing, and it is expedient and necessary therefore that they should be propitiated so that their evil influence may be removed and the thing itself may prosper. These doubles are not as yet gods, they are merely powers, potentialities, but in the course of time they develop into gods. The first step in this direction is the obtaining of a *name,* a name the knowledge of which gives a certain control over the power to him who knows it. Finally these powers equipped with a name begin to take on personal characteristics, to be thought of as individuals, and finally represented under the form of men.

It cannot be shown that all the gods of Rome originated in this way, but certainly many of them did, and it is not impossible that they all did; and this theory of their origin explains better than any other theory certain habits of thought which the early Romans cherished in regard to their gods. At the time when our knowledge of Roman religion begins, Rome is in possession of a great many gods, but very few of them are much more than names for powers. They are none of them personal enough to be connected together in myths. And this is the very simple reason why there was no such thing as [Pg 7] a native Roman mythology, a blank in Rome's early development which many modern writers have refused to admit, taking upon themselves the unnecessary trouble of positing an original mythology later lost. The gods of early Rome were neither married nor given in marriage; they had no children or grandchildren and there were no divine genealogies. Instead they were thought of occasionally as more or less individual powers, but usually as masses of potentialities, grouped together for convenience as the "gods of the country," the "gods of the storeroom," the "gods of the dead," etc. Even when they were conceived of as somewhat individual, they were usually very closely associated with the corresponding object, for example Vesta was not so much the goddess of the hearth as the goddess "Hearth" itself, Janus not the god of doors so much as the god "Door."

But by just as much as the human element was absent from the concept of the deity, by just so much the element of formalism in the cult was greater. This formalism must not be interpreted according to our modern ideas; it was not a formalism which was the result and the successor of a decadent spirituality; it was not a secondary product in an age of the decline of faith; but it was itself the essence of religion in the period of the greatest religious purity. In the careful and conscientious fulfilment of the form consisted the whole [Pg

8] duty of man toward his gods. Such a state of affairs would have been intolerable in any nation whose instincts were less purely legal. So identical were the laws concerning the gods and the laws concerning men that though in the earliest period of Roman jurisprudence the *ius divinum* and the *ius humanum* are already separated, they are separated merely formally as two separate fields or provinces in which the spirit of the law and often even the letter of its enactment are the same. Such a formalism implies a very firm belief in the existence of the gods. The dealings of a man with the gods are quite as really reciprocal as his dealings with his fellow citizens. But on the other hand though the existence of the gods is never doubted for a moment, the gods themselves are an unknown quantity; hence out of the formal relationship an intimacy never developed, and while it is scarcely just to characterise the early cult as exclusively a religion of fear, certainly real affection is not present until a much later day. The potentiality of the gods always overshadowed their personality. But this was not all loss, for the absence of personality prevented the growth of those gross myths which are usually found among primitive peoples, for the purer more inspiring myths of gods are not the primitive product but result from the process of refining which accompanies a people's growth in culture. Thus the theory of animism illumines the religious condition of that borderland [Pg 9] of history in which Romulus and Numa Pompilius have their dwelling-place.

According to that pleasant fiction of which the ancient world was so extremely fond—the belief that all institutions could be traced back to their establishment by some individual—the religion of Rome was supposed to have been founded by her second king Numa, and it was the custom to refer to all that was most antique in the cult as forming a part of the venerable "religion of Numa." For us this can be merely a name, and even as a name misleading, for a part of the beliefs with which we are dealing go back for centuries before Romulus and the traditional B.C. 753 as the foundation of Rome. But it is a convenient term if we mean by it merely the old kingdom before foreign influences began to work. The Romans of a later time coined an excellent name not so much for the period as for the kind of religion which existed then, contrasting the original deities of Rome with the new foreign gods, calling the former the "old indigenous gods" (*Di Indigetes*) and the latter the "newly settled gods" (*Di Novensides*). For our knowledge of the religion of this period we are not dependent upon a mere theory, no matter how good it may be in itself, but we have the best sort of contemporary evidence in addition, and it is to the discovery of this evidence that the modern study of Roman religion virtually owes its existence. The records of early political [Pg 10] history were largely destroyed in B.C. 390 when the Gauls sacked Rome, but the religious status, with the conservativeness characteristic of religion generally, suffered very few changes during all these years, and left a record of itself in the annually recurring festivals of the Roman year, festivals which grew into an instinctive function of the life of the common people. Many centuries later when the calendar was engraved on stone, these revered old festivals were inscribed on these stone calendars in peculiarly large letters as distinguished from all the other items. Thus from the fragments of these stone calendars, which have been found, and which are themselves nineteen centuries old, we can read back another eight or ten centuries further. By the aid of this "calendar of Numa" we are able to assert the presence of certain deities in the Rome of this time, and the equally important absence of others. And from the character of the deities present and of the festivals themselves a correct and more or less detailed picture of the religious condition of the time may be drawn. This calendar and the list of *Indigetes* extracted from it form the foundation for all our study of the history of Roman religion.

The religious forms of a community are always so bound up with its social organisation that a satisfactory knowledge of the one is practically impossible without some knowledge of the other. Unfortunately there is no field in Roman history [Pg 11] where theories are so abundant and facts so rare as in regard to the question of the early social organisation. But without coming into conflict with any of the rival theories we may make at least the following statements. In the main the community was fairly uniform and homogeneous, there were no great social extremes and no conspicuous foreign element, so that each individual, had he stopped to analyse his social position, would have found himself in four distinct relationships: a relationship to himself as an individual; to his family; to the group of families which formed his clan (*gens*); and finally to the state. We may go a step further on safe ground and assert that the least important of these relations was that to himself, and the most important that to his family. The unit of early Roman social life was not the individual but the family, and in the most primitive ideas of life after death it is the family which has immortality, not the individual. The state is not a union of individuals but of families. The very psychological idea of the individual seems to have taken centuries to develop, and to have reached its real significance only under the empire. Of the four elements therefore we have established the pre-eminence of the family and the importance of the state as based on the family idea; the individual may be disregarded in this early period, and there is left only the clan, which however offers a difficult problem. The family and the [Pg 12] state were destined to hold their own, merely exchanging places in the course of time, so that the state came first and the family second; the individual was to grow into ever increasing importance, but the clan is already dying when history begins. It is a pleasant theory and one that has a high degree of probability that there may have been a time when the clan was to the family what the state is when history begins, and that when the state arose out of a union of various clans, the immediate allegiance of each family was gradually alienated from its clan and transferred to the state, so that the clan gave up its life in order that the state, the child of its own creation, might live. If this be so, we can see why the social importance of the clan ceases so early in Roman history.

The centre therefore of early religious life is the family, and the state as a macrocosm of the family; and the father of each family is its chief priest, and the king as the father of the state is the chief priest of the state. As for the individual the only god which he has for worship is his "double," called in the case of a man his *Genius* and in that of a woman her *Juno*, her individualisation of the goddess Juno, quite a distinct deity, peculiar to herself. But even here the family instinct shows itself, and though later the Genius and the Juno represent all that is intellectual in the individual, they seem originally to have symbolised the procreative power of the individual in rela [Pg 13] tion to the continuance of the family. The family and the state, however, side by side worshipped a number of deities.

In the primitive hut, the model of which has come down to us in so many little burial urns of early time (for example those that have recently been dug up in the wonderful cemetery under the Roman Forum), with its one door and no window, there were several elements which needed propitiation; the door itself as the keeper away of evil, the hearth, and the niche for the storage of food. The door-god was the god-door Janus, the *ianua* itself; the hearth was in the care of the womenfolk, the wife and daughters, so it was a goddess, Vesta, whom they served; and the storage-niche, the *penus*, was in the keeping of the "store-closet gods" (*Di Penates*). The state itself was modelled after the house. It had its Janus, its sacred door, down in the Forum, and the king himself, the father of the state, was his special priest; it had its hearth, where the sacred fire burned, and its own Vesta, tended by the vestal virgins, the daughters of the state; and it had its store-niche with its Penates. At a later date but still very early there was added to the household worship the idea of the general protector of the house, the Lar, which gave rise to the familiar expression "Lares and Penates." The origin of this *Lar Familiaris*, as he is called, is interesting, because it shows the intimate connection [Pg 14] between the farming life of the community and its religion. The Lares were originally the group of gods who looked after the various farms; they were in the plural because they were worshipped where the boundary lines of several farms met, but though several of them were worshipped together, each farm had its one individual Lar. But the care of the farm included also the protection of the house on the farm, so that the Lar of the farm became also the Lar of the house, first of course of houses on farms, and then of every house everywhere even when no farm was connected with it.

Aside from Vesta, the Genius, the Lar, and the Penates, possibly the most important element in family worship was the cult of the dead ancestors. This cult is, of course, common to almost all religions, and its presence in Roman religion is in so far not surprising, but the form in which it occurs there is curious and relatively rare. Just as the living man has a "double," the Genius, so the dead man also must have a double, but this double is originally not the Genius, who seems to have been thought of at first as ceasing with the individual. On the contrary as death is the great leveller and the remover of individuality, so the double of the dead was not thought of at first as an individual double but merely as forming a part of an indefinite mass of spirits, the "good gods" (*Di Manes*) as they were called because they were feared as being anything but good. These [Pg 15] *Di Manes* had therefore no specific relation to the individual, and the individual really ceased at death; the only human relation which the *Di Manes* seem to have preserved was a connection with the living members of the family to which they had originally belonged. It is therefore very misleading to assert that the Romans had from the beginning a belief in immortality, when we instinctively think of the immortality of the individual. The thing that was immortal was not the individual but the family. It is thoroughly in keeping with the practical character of the Roman mind that they did not concern themselves with the place in which these spirits of the dead were supposed to reside, but merely with the door through which they could and did return to earth. We have no accounts of the Lower World until Greece lent her mythology to Rome, and imagination never built anything like the Greek palace of Pluto. But while they did not waste energy in furnishing the Lower World with the fittings of fancy, they did keep a careful guard over the door of egress. This door they called the *mundus*, and represented it crudely by a trench or shallow pit, at the bottom of which there lay a stone. On certain days of the year this stone was removed, and then the spirits came back to earth again, where they were received and entertained by the living members of their family. There were a number of these days in the year, three of them scattered through the [Pg 16] year: August 24, October 5, November 8; and two sets of days: February 13-21 and May 9, 11, 13. The February celebration, the so-called *Parentalia*, was calm and dignified and represented all that was least superstitious and fearful in the generally terrifying worship of the dead. The *Lemuria* in May had exactly the opposite character and belongs to the category of the "expulsion of evil spirits," of which Mr. Frazer in his *Golden Bough* has given so many instances.

In this connection it is interesting to notice two facts which stand almost as corollaries to these beliefs. One fact is the religious necessity for the continuance of the family, in order that there might always be a living representative of the family to perform the sacrifices to the ancestors. It was the duty of the head of the family not only to perform these sacrifices himself as long as he lived but also to provide a successor. The usual method was by marriage and the rearing of a family, but, in case there was no male child in the family, adoption was recurred to. Here it is peculiarly significant that the sanction of the chief priest was necessary, and he never gave his consent in case the man to be adopted was the only representative of his family, so that his removal from that family into another would leave his original family without a male representative. In cases of inheritance the first lien on the income was for the maintenance of the traditional sacrifices [Pg 17] unless some special arrangement had been made. These exceptional inheritances, without the deduction for sacrifices, were naturally desired above all others and the phrase "an inheritance without sacrifices" (*hereditas sine sacris*) became by degrees the popular expression for a godsend. The other fact of interest in this connection is that, inasmuch as ancestors were worshipped only *en masse* and not as individuals, that process could not take place in Roman religion which is so familiar in many other religions, namely that the great gods of the state should some of them have been originally ancestors whose greatness during life had produced a corresponding emphasis in their worship after death, so that ultimately they were promoted from the ranks of the deified dead into the select Olympus of individual gods. This has been a favourite theory of the making of a god from the time of Euhemerus down to Herbert Spencer. There are religions in which it is true for certain of the major gods, but there are no traces of the process in Roman religion, and the reason is obvious in view of the peculiar character of ancestor worship in Rome.

We have now seen the principal elements which went to make up the family religion and that part of the state religion which was an enlargement and an imitation of the family religion. But even in the most primitive times a Roman's life was not bounded by his own hut and the phenomenon of death. There [Pg 18] was work to be done in life, a living to be gained, and here, as everywhere, there were hosts of unseen powers who must be propitiated. His religion was not only coincident with every phase of private life, it was also closely related to the specific occupations and interests of the people, and just as the interests of the community, its means of livelihood, were agriculture and stock-raising, so the gods were those of the crops and the herds. Some years ago the late Professor Mommsen succeeded in extracting from the existing stone calendars a list of the religious festivals of the old Roman year, and also in proving that this list of festivals was complete in its present condition at a time before the city of Rome was surrounded by the wall which Servius Tullius built, and that it therefore goes back to the old kingdom, the time of what has been called the "Religion of Numa." We cannot go through all the festivals in detail, but it is extremely interesting to notice that almost every one of them is connected with the life of the farmer and represents the action of propitiation towards some god or group of gods at every time in the Roman year which was at all critical for agricultural interests.

It must not be forgotten also that this list is not absolutely complete, because it represents merely the official state festivals, and not even all of them but only those which fell upon the same day or days every year, so that they could be engraved in the stone to [Pg 19] form a perpetual calendar. All state festivals, of which there were several, which were appointed in each particular year according to the backward or forward estate of the harvest, were omitted from the list, though they were celebrated at some time in every year; and naturally the public calendars contained no reference to the many private and semi-private ceremonies of the year, with which the state had nothing official to do, festivals of the family and the clan, and even local festivals of various districts of the city.

In this list of peaceful deities of the farm there is one god whose character has been very much misunderstood because of the company which he keeps; this is the god Mars. It has become the fashion of late to consider him as a god of vegetation, and a great many ingenious arguments have been brought forward to show his agricultural character. But the more primitive a community is, the more intense is its struggle for existence, and the more rife its rivalries with its neighbours. Alongside of the ploughshare there must always have been the sword or its equivalent, and along with Flora and Ceres there must always have been a god of strife and battle. That Mars was this god in early as well as later times is shown above all things by the fact that he was always worshipped outside the city, as a god who must be kept at a distance. Naturally his cult was associated with the dominant interest of [Pg 20] life, the crops, and he was worshipped in the beautiful ceremony of the purification of the fields, which Mr. Walter Pater has so exquisitely described at the opening of *Marius the Epicurean*. But he was regarded as the protector of the fields and the warder off of evil influences rather than as a positive factor in the development of the crops. Then too in the early days of the Roman militia, before the regular army had come into existence, the war season was only during the summer after the planting and before the harvest, so that the two festivals which marked the beginning and the end of that season were also readily associated with the state of the crops at that time.

But the most interesting and curious thing about this old religion is not so much what it does contain as what it does not. It is not so much what we find as what we miss, for more than half the gods whom we instinctively associate with Rome were not there under this old regime. Here is a partial list of those whose names we do not find: Minerva, Diana, Venus, Fortuna, Hercules, Castor, Pollux, Apollo, Mercury, Dis, Proserpina, Aesculapius, the Magna Mater. And yet their absence is not surprising when we realise that almost all of the gods in this list represent phases of life with which Rome in this early period was absolutely unacquainted. She had no appreciable trade or commerce, no manufactures or particular handicrafts, and no political interests except the [Pg 21] simple patriarchal government which sufficed for her present needs. Her gods of water were the gods of rivers and springs; Neptune was there, but he was not the ocean-god like the Greek Poseidon. Vulcan, the god of fire, who was afterwards associated with the Greek Hephaistos and became the patron of metal-working, was at this time merely the god of destructive and not of constructive fire. Even the great god Juppiter who was destined to become almost identical with the name and fame of Rome was not yet a god of the state and politics, but merely the sky-god, especially the lightning god, Juppiter Feretrius, the "striker," who had a little shrine on the Capitoline where later the great Capitoline temple of Juppiter Optimus Maximus was to stand. Another curious characteristic of this early age, which, I think, has never been commented on, is the extraordinarily limited number of goddesses. Vesta is the only one who seems to stand by herself without a male parallel. Each of the others is merely the contrasted potentiality in a pair of which the male is much more famous, and the only ones in these pairs who ever obtained a pronounced individuality did so because their cult was afterwards reinforced by being associated with some extra-Roman cult. The best illustration of this last is Juno. We may go further and say that it-seems highly probable that the worship of female deities was in the main confined to the women of the community, while the [Pg 22] men worshipped the gods. This distinction extended even to the priesthoods where the wife of the priest of a god was the priestess of the corresponding goddess. Such a state of affairs is doubly interesting in view of the pre-eminence of female deities in the early Greek world, which has been so strikingly shown by Miss Jane Harrison in her recent book, *Prolegomena to the Study of Greek Religion*.

The most vital question which can be put to almost any religion is that in regard to its expansive power and its adaptability to new conditions. Society is bound to undergo changes, and a young social organism, if normal, is continually growing new cells. New conditions are arising and new interests are coming to the front. In addition, if the growth is to be continuous, new material is being constantly absorbed, and the simple homogeneous character of the old society is being entirely changed by the influx of foreign elements. This is what occurred in ancient Rome, and it is because ancient Roman religion was not capable of organic development from within, that the curious things happened to it which our history has to record. It is these strange external accretions which lend the chief interest to the story, while at the same time they conceal the original form so fully as to render the writing of a history of Roman religion extremely difficult.

Yet it must not be supposed because Roman [Pg 23] religion was unable to adapt itself to the new constitution of society with its contrasted classes, and to the new commercial and political interests which attracted the attention of the upper classes, that it was absolutely devoid within itself, within its own limitations, of a certain capability of development. For several centuries after outside influences began to affect Rome, her original religion kept on developing alongside of the new forms. The manner in which it developed is thoroughly significant of the original national character of the Romans.

We have seen that from the very beginning the nature of the gods as powers rather than personalities tended to emphasise the value and importance of the name, which usually indicated the particular function or speciality of each deity and was very often the only thing known about him. In the course of time as the original name of the deity began to be thought of entirely as a proper name without any meaning, rather than as a common noun explaining the nature of the god to which it was attached, it became necessary to add to the original name some adjective which would adequately describe the god and do the work which the name by itself had originally done. And as the nature of the various deities grew more complicated along with the increasing complications of daily life, new adjectives were added, each one expressing some particular phase of the god's activity. Such an [Pg 24] adjective was called a *cognomen*, and was often of very great importance because it began to be felt that a god with one adjective, *i.e.* invoked for one purpose, was almost a different god from the same god with a different adjective, *i.e.* invoked for another purpose. Thus a knowledge of these adjectives was almost as necessary as a knowledge of the name of the god. The next step in the development was one which followed very easily. These important adjectives began to be thought of as having a value and an existence in themselves, apart from the god to which they were attached. The grammatical change which accompanied this psychological movement was the transfer of the adjective into an abstract noun. Both adjectives and abstract nouns express quality, but the adjective is in a condition of dependence on a noun, while the abstract noun is independent and self-supporting. And thus, just as in certain of the lower organisms a group of cells breaks off and sets up an individual organism of its own, so in old Roman religion some phase of a god's activity, expressed in an adjective, broke off with the adjective from its original stock and set up for itself, turning its name from the dependent adjective form into the independent abstract noun. Thus Juppiter, worshipped as a god of good faith in the dealings of men with one another, the god by whom oaths were sworn under the open sky, was designated as "Juppiter, guarding-good-faith," [Pg 25] Juppiter Fidius. There were however many other phases of Juppiter's work, and hence the adjective *fidius* became very important as the means of distinguishing this activity from all the others. Eventually it broke off from Juppiter and formed the abstract noun *Fides*, the goddess of good faith, where the sex of the deity as a goddess was entirely determined by the grammatical gender of abstract nouns as feminine.

This is all strange enough but there is one more step in the development even more curious yet. This abstract goddess *Fides* did not stay long in the purely abstract sphere; she began very soon to be made concrete again, as the Fides of this particular person or of that particular group and as this Fides or that, until she became almost as concrete as Juppiter himself had been, and hence we have a great many different *Fides* in seeming contradiction to the old grammatical rule that abstract nouns had no plural. Now all this development in the field of religion throws light upon the character of the Roman mind and its instinctive methods of thought, and we see why it is that the Romans were very great lawyers and very mediocre philosophers. Both law and philosophy require the ability for abstract thought; in both cases the essential qualities of a thing must be separated from the thing itself. But in the case of philosophic thought this abstraction, these qualities, do not immediately seek rein [Pg 26] carnation. They continue as abstractions and do not immediately descend to earth again, whereas for law such a descent is absolutely necessary because jurisprudence is interested not so much in the abstraction by itself, but rather in the abstract as presented in concrete cases. Hence a type of mind which found it equally easy to make the concrete into the abstract and then to turn the abstract so made into a kind of concrete again, is *par excellence* the legal mind, and no better proof of the instinctive tendency to law-making on the part of the Romans can be found than in the fact that the same habits of mind which make laws also governed the development of their religion.

Unfortunately however it was not these abstract deities who could save old Roman religion. They were merely the logical outcome of the deities already existing, merely new offspring of the old breed. They did not represent any new interests, but were merely the individualisation of certain phases of the old deities, phases which had always been present and were now at most merely emphasised by being worshipped separately.

[Pg 27]

THE REORGANISATION OF SERVIUS

Like a lofty peak rising above the mists which cover the tops of the lower-lying mountains, the figure of Servius Tullius towers above the semi-legendary Tarquins on either side of him. We feel that we have to do with a veritable character in history, and we find ourselves wondering what sort of a man he was personally—a feeling that never occurs to us with Romulus and the older kings, and comes to us only faintly with the elder Tarquin, while the younger Tarquin has all the marks of a wooden man, who was put up only to be thrown down, whose whole *raison d'être* is to explain the transition from the kingdom to the republic on the theory of a revolution. Eliminate the revolution, suppose the change to have been a gradual and a constitutional one, and you may discard the proud Tarquin without losing anything but a lay-figure with its more or less gaudy trappings of later myths. But it is not so with Servius; his wall and his constitution are very real and defy all attempts to turn their maker into a legend. Yet on the other hand we [Pg 28] must be on our guard, for much of the definiteness which seems to attach to him is rather the definiteness of a certain stage in Rome's development, a certain well-bounded chronological and sociological tract. It is dangerous to try to limit too strictly Servius's personal part in this development; and far safer, though perhaps less fascinating, to use his name as a general term for the changes which Rome underwent from the time when foreign influences began to tell upon her until the beginning of the republic. He forms a convenient title therefore for certain phases of Rome's growth. And yet even this is not strictly correct, for Servius stands not so much for the coming into existence of certain facts, as for the recognition of the existence of these facts. The facts themselves were of slow growth, covering probably centuries, but the actions resulting from them, and the outward changes in society, came thick and fast and may well have taken place, all of them, within the limits of one man's life. The foundation fact upon which all these changes were based is the influence of the outside world on the Roman community. Until this time there had been little to differentiate Rome from any other of the hill-communities of Italy, of which there were scores in her immediate neighbourhood; nor was she the only one to come into contact with the outside world. It was the effect which that influence had upon her as contrasted with her neighbours which [Pg 29] made the difference. When we ask why this influence affected her differently we find no satisfactory answer, and are in the presence of a mystery—the world-old insoluble mystery of the superiority of one tribe or one individual over others apparently of the same class. Political history is wont to tell this chapter of Rome's story under the title of the "Rise of the Plebeians," but the presence of the Plebeians was only the outward symbol of an inward change. This change was the breaking up of the monotonous one-class society of the primitive community with its one—agricultural—interest, and the formation of a variegated many-class society with manifold interests, such as trade, handicraft, and politics. It was the awakening of Rome into a world-life out of her century-long undisturbed bucolic slumber.

There were at this time two peoples in Italy, who by reason of their older culture were able to be Rome's teachers. One lay to the north of her, the mysterious Etruscans, whose culture fortunately for Rome had only a very moderate influence, because the Etruscan culture had already lost much of its virility, possibly also because it was distinctly felt to be foreign, and hence could effect no insidious entry, and probably because Rome was at this time too strong and young and clean to take anything but the best from Etruria. The other lay to the south, the Greek colonies of Magna Graecia, separated from Rome for the present by many miles of forest and [Pg 30] by hostile tribes. Around her in Latium were her own next of kin, the Latins, becoming rapidly inferior to her, but enabled to do her at least this service, that of absorbing the foreign influences which came, and in certain cases latinising them, and thus transmitting them to Rome in a more or less assimilated condition.

The three great facts in the life of Rome during this period are the coming of Greek merchants and Greek trade from the south, the coming of Etruscan artisans and handicraft from the north, and the beginnings of her political rivalry and gradual prominence in the league of Latin cities around her. Each one of these movements is reflected in the religious changes of the period. In regard to the first two this is not surprising, for the ancient traveller, like his mythical prototype Aeneas, carried his gods with him. Thus there were worshipped in private in Rome the gods of all the peoples who settled within her walls, and the presence of these gods was destined to make its influence felt. Your primitive polytheist is very catholic in his religious tastes; for, when one is already in possession of many gods, the addition of a few more is a minor matter, especially when, as was now the case in Rome, these deities are the patrons of occupations and interests hitherto entirely unknown to the Roman, and hence not provided for in his scheme of gods. It was therefore in no spirit of disloyalty to the [Pg 31] already existing gods, and with no desire to introduce rival deities, that the new cults began to spread until they became so important as to call for state recognition.

Possibly the most interesting cases are those of the two gods who came from the south, Hercules and Castor, interesting because they were the forerunners of that great multitude of Greek gods who later came in proudly by special invitation, and even more interesting yet because, though they were Greek as Greek could be, they came into Rome, as it were, incognito, and were so far from being known as Greek, that, when the same gods came in afterwards more directly, these new-comers were felt to be quite a different thing, and their worship was carried on in another part of the city away from the old-established cults.

In the Greek world Herakles and Hermes were the especial patrons of travellers, and as travelling was never done for pleasure but always for business, they became the patrons of the travelling merchant. It was also natural that they should go with the settlers away from the mother-city into the new colony. Thus it was that they came from the mother-land into the colonies of Magna Graecia in Southern Italy, and once being established there made their way slowly but inevitably northwards. The story of Hermes, under the name of Mercury, belongs to a later chapter, but that of Herakles = [Pg 32] Hercules must be recounted here. It is only within the last few years that the scholarly world has been persuaded that there was no such thing as an original Italic Hercules; at first sight it was very difficult to believe, because there seemed to be so many apparently very old Italic legends centering in Hercules. But it has been shown, either that these legends never existed and rest solely upon false interpretation of monuments, or that, though they did exist at an early date, they were introduced under Greek influence. It was the trading merchant therefore who brought Herakles northward. And as the god went, his name was softened into Hercules, and with the assimilation of the name to the tongue of the Italic people, there went hand in hand an adaptation of his nature to their needs, so that by degrees he became thoroughly italicised both in form and content. It is probable that the cult came into Rome as well as into the other cities of Latium, but in Rome it was confined to a few individuals, and at first obtained no public recognition. On the contrary, for reasons that we are at a loss to find, this Greek cult seems to have reached very large proportions in the little town of Tibur (Tivoli), fourteen miles north-east of Rome. There it dominated all other worship and lost so much of its foreign atmosphere that it became thoroughly latinised. In the course of time the Roman state acknowledged this Tivoli cult of Hercules and [Pg 33] accepted a branch of it as its own. But the extraordinary thing about this acknowledgment is that the Romans felt it to be a Latin and not a foreign cult. They showed this intimate and friendly feeling by permitting an altar to Hercules to be erected within the city proper, in the Forum Boarium. But in order to understand the significance of this act a word of digression is necessary.

Under the old Roman regime every act of life was performed under the supervision of the gods, and this godly patronage was especially emphasised in acts which affected the life of the community. No act was of greater importance for the community than the choice of a home, the location of a settlement. Thus the founding of an ancient city was accompanied by sacred rites, chief among which was the ploughing of a furrow around the space which was ultimately to be enclosed by the wall. This furrow formed a symbolic wall on very much the same principle as that on which the witch draws her circle. The furrow was called the *pomerium* and was to the world of the gods what the city wall was to the world of men. It did not however always coincide with the actual city wall, and the space it embraced was sometimes less, sometimes more, than that embraced by the city wall; and just as new walls covering larger territory could be built for the city, so a new *pomerium* line could be drawn. As was becoming for a spiritual barrier there was nothing to mark it [Pg 34] except the boundary stones through which the imaginary line passed. The wall, which Servius built and which continued to be the outer wall of Rome for a period of eight or nine hundred years until the third Christian century, was at the time of its building coincident in the main with the line of the *pomerium*, with one very important exception: namely that all the region of the Aventine, which was inside the limits of the political city and embraced by the Servian wall, lay outside the *pomerium* line and was in other words outside the religious city. It continued thus all through the republic and into the empire until the reign of Claudius. Originally the *pomerium* line played an important part in the religious world and it continued to do so until the middle of the republic, during the Second Punic War, when its sanctity was destroyed and it lost its real religious significance, though it remained as a formal institution. As a divine barrier it served originally in the world of the gods very much the same purpose as the material wall of stone did in the world of men. Before the problem of foreign gods had begun to exist for the Romans, in the good old days when they knew only the gods of their own religion, the *pomerium* served to keep within the bounds of Rome all the beneficent kindly gods whose presence was not needed outside in the fields, and it served fully as important a purpose in keeping outside of Rome the gods who [Pg 35] were feared rather than loved, for example the dread war-god Mars. When foreign gods began to be introduced into Rome they might, of course, be worshipped inside the *pomerium* by private individuals, but when the state acknowledged them it was more prudent that her worship should be outside the sacred wall. Thus it came to pass that the foreign gods, who were taken into the cult of the Roman state, were given temples in the Campus Martius or over on the Aventine, and the two or three cases where they were publicly worshipped inside the *pomerium* form no real exception to this rule—such an exception would be, in fact, quite unthinkable in the strictly logical system of Roman worship—but these gods were allowed inside because they came to Rome from her kinsfolk, the Latins, and were not felt to be foreign.

Hercules is one of the cases in this last category. Though originally, as we have seen, a Greek god, his long residence in Tibur (Tivoli) had made him, as it were, a naturalised citizen of Latium, and hence Rome felt it no impropriety to take him inside her *pomerium*. At first his worship seems to have been carried on by two clans, the Potitii and the Pinarii, but later, during the republic, the state assumed control. But though it was really the Greek Herakles who had come in as the latinised Hercules, the god had paid a certain price for his admission, for he came stripped of all the various attributes which he had had [Pg 36] in Greece and retaining merely his function as patron of trade and travel. It was this practical side of his nature alone which appealed to the Romans; it found its expression in the offering of "the tenth" at the great altar in the Forum Boarium. This altar always remained in a certain sense the centre of Hercules-worship in Rome. It was reinforced at an early date by no less than three temples of Hercules in the more or less immediate neighbourhood, all of which were characterised by the same relative simplicity of ritual. Centuries later Herakles became known to the Romans through direct Greek channels, and it was recognised that this new Herakles was akin to the old Hercules, so that he too was called Hercules. There was nothing surprising in this to the Romans, because they considered it a matter of course that there should be found a parallel among their own gods for each Greek deity. They never understood the true state of affairs; it is doubtful whether they could have understood it: namely, that in almost all their other identifications of Roman and Greek deities, they were really doing violence to their own native gods by superimposing upon them the attributes of a deity with whom they had really nothing in common, whereas, in identifying the new Herakles with their old Hercules, they were doing a perfectly legitimate thing. For one who knows the true state of affairs there is something pathetically amusing in the fact [Pg 37] that they really showed more delicacy in making their old (really originally Greek) Hercules into the new Greek Herakles-Hercules, than they did in throwing together Neptune and Poseidon, Mars and Ares, Diana and Artemis. As a matter of fact they always reverenced the old cult of the great altar, and never allowed the more sensational phases of Greek worship to be practised there, and put off into another quarter the temples which were built to Hercules under the various new attributes which the new Greek cult brought with it. These temples were placed, as was proper, outside the *pomerium*, in the southern part of the Campus Martius.

But to return to the simple Hercules and the Servian regime, the Roman state had now obtained a deity, of which, by the contagion of commerce, they already felt a need, a god of great power from whom came success in the practical undertakings of life. Hence he had a strong hold on the Romans whose practical side was undergoing a rapid development. The idea of trade was now represented in the religious world, it had received its divine sanction.

The other god, who came up from Magna Graecia and whose formal acceptance into the state-cult formed one of the earliest incidents in the breakdown of the old agricultural religion, was Castor, with his twin-brother Pollux, although brother Pollux was always an insignificant partner, so much so that the temple which was subsequently built to them both [Pg 38] was referred to either as the temple of "Castor" alone or as the temple of "the Castors." At various points in the old Greek world we meet with a pair of brothers, at first not designated by individual names but merely named as a pair. Even these pair-names do not agree, but they represent all of them the same idea. Later when individual names are substituted for the general pair-name, these individual names also differ. They are gods of protection, and on the sea-coast—and most of Greece is sea-coast—they are especially helpful as rescuers from the dangers of the sea, and they are also very early and almost everywhere connected with horses. But in spite of their usefulness they are not very prominent, and it is doubtful whether they would ever have become famous, except for one of those little accidents which make the fortunes of gods as well as of men. It so happened that horses began to be used in warfare more than for the mere drawing of chariots; a primitive sort of cavalry came into being, produced by mounting heavy-armed foot-soldiers on horseback. With this cavalry the "Twin-Brothers" (*Dios-kouroi* = "Sons of Zeus"), especially Castor, became prominent. Just as the Greek merchants had taken Herakles with them when they set out to plant colonies in Southern Italy, so the heavy-mounted horsemen carried their god Castor with them wherever they went. The Italic tribes in their turn were quick to seize upon [Pg 39] this idea of cavalry, and with it as an essential part went its divine patron, Castor. Thus the Castor-cult moved steadily northward, carried, as it were, on horseback. At last it reached Latium, and there the little town of Tusculum, afterwards so famous as the residence of Cicero, became in some unaccountable way an important cult-centre, and did for Castor what Tibur had done for Hercules, *i.e.* latinised him, so that Rome received him not as an alien but as one of her kin. There can be little doubt that the Roman cult actually did come from Tusculum, and that in its introduction into Rome, as in every other step on its march, it was connected with the reorganisation of the cavalry. This would seem to imply that Tusculum was famous for its cavalry and that Rome took the idea of it from her—statements for which we have unfortunately no other confirmation, though we have abundant proof of the cult at Tusculum and of Rome's close association with it.

Castor was thus the patron of the "horsemen" (*equites*) and his great day was July 15, when the horsemen's parade took place. Possibly this had been the date of the festival at Tusculum, a day especially appropriate because it was the Ides of the month, and the Ides were sacred to Juppiter, whose sons Castor and Pollux (*Dios-kouroi*) were supposed to be. It is extremely interesting in the light of this knowledge of the true state of affairs to see how [Pg 40] legend later explained the coming of Castor and Pollux. It was an incident in the mythical war which was supposed to have taken place after the last Tarquin had been driven out, and the republic had been started. The adversaries of Rome, allied with Tarquin, notably Octavius Mamilius of Tusculum, fought against the Romans in the battle of Lake Regillus on July 15, B.C. 499. The Romans won, and the first news of victory was brought to Rome by the miraculous appearance of Castor and Pollux who were seen watering their horses in the Forum at the spring of Juturna. A temple on this spot was then vowed and fifteen years later, B.C. 484, it was completed and dedicated. Tusculum, July 15, and the dedication of the temple in B.C. 484 are seemingly the only historical facts in this legend; and long before B.C. 499 Castor was worshipped in Rome, especially on July 15. The site of his original worship was without doubt the same locality in the Forum where his temple was subsequently built, for it is an almost invariable rule that the earliest temples are built on the actual site of, or close to, the old altar or shrine which preceded the formal temple. Like Hercules therefore he was received inside the *pomerium*, and probably for a similar reason, because it was felt that he was a god of Tusculum, and hence a god of Rome's kinsfolk. We have an additional confirmation of this feeling in the way in which the later direct cult of Castor [Pg 41] was treated. This cult, connecting Castor with healing and the interpretation of dreams, and emphasising his function as a rescuer from the dangers of the sea, would have been without meaning for the old Romans who worshipped him merely as a patron of horsemen and horsemanship. The new ideas seem to have had as their centre a later temple in the Circus Flaminius and thus Hercules and Castor may again be paralleled, since they have, each of them, an old cult-centre inside the *pomerium*, Hercules in the Forum Boarium, Castor in the Forum, and a later cult-centre, for more advanced ideas, in each case in the Circus Flaminius.

Although it was Greek influence which ultimately caused the destruction of Roman religion, and although the cults of Hercules and of Castor are the first definite effects of this influence, it cannot be said that the destruction had in any sense begun, because in their slow journey northward, and in their long residence at Tibur and Tusculum respectively, the two cults had lost all that was pernicious. The Roman instinct, which felt them to be akin to itself, did not go amiss; they were indeed akin to the new Rome with its new interest in trade and its increased interest in warfare, for the trader and the warrior have gone side by side in all ages of the world's history, whether it be a primitive instinct to grasp territory for commercial purposes or a more civilised endeavour to obtain an open port. [Pg 42]

The beginnings of Greek influence have thus been exhibited in the case of Hercules and of Castor, and it remains to inquire what Etruria did. There is no race about which we know so much and yet so little as about the Etruscans. They have always been and still are a riddle, and as our knowledge of them increases we seem further than ever from a solution, and what we gain in positive knowledge is more than counterbalanced by the increased sense of our ignorance. Altogether aside from the problem of the origin of the Etruscans, and the race to which they belonged, is the other problem of their disappearance. In a certain sense Etruria steps out of history quite as mysteriously as she entered into it, nay even more mysteriously, for we are always willing to allow a certain percentage of mystery as the legitimate accompaniment of prehistoric history, but when in the light of more or less historic times a nation steps off the stage of the world's history, and leaves practically no heritage behind her, we have a right to be amazed. Of all the peoples in Italy

Rome ought in the order of events to have been her successor, and yet when we contrast the influence of Etruria on Rome with the influence of the Greek colonies of Southern Italy we see an amazing difference. The influence of these Greek colonies on Rome prepared the way for the direct influence of the Greek motherland, so that one passed over into the other by imperceptible [Pg 43] gradations, but the influence of Etruria on Rome not only led to nothing but was in itself of a most superficial sort. Etruria must have had some literature, yet we search the history of Roman literature in vain for any traces of the influence of that literature on Rome, with the one exception of books on divination and the interpretation of lightning. We know too little of her manners and customs to be able to tell exactly how much they may have influenced Rome, and yet it is worth noting that the things which Roman writers actually refer to Etruria, are all of them most superficial: a few of the insignia of political office; a few of the trappings of one or two ritualistic acts; a branch of divination, by the consultation of the entrails (*haruspicina*), which was of secondary importance compared to augury; and the most depraved form of Roman public sport, the gladiatorial games. The only fundamental institution of Rome which it is the habit to ascribe to Etruria, the idea of the so-called *templum* or division of the sky into regions as an axiom of augury, seems to have been quite as much a general Italic idea as a specifically Etruscan one. Even in art her influence was relatively slight, and though her architects seem to have built the earliest formal temples for Rome, they were soon succeeded in this work by the Greeks. We seek in vain for a complete and satisfactory explanation of this limitation of her influence, but certain thoughts suggest them [Pg 44] selves, which, as far as they go, are probably correct. All that we know of Etruria impresses us with the fact that hers was an outward civilisation unaccompanied by an inward culture, that it was a formal rather than a spiritual growth, an artificial acquisition from without rather than a development from within outwards. It was strong but with its strength went brutality, it was interested in art but for its sensual rather than its spiritual aspects. Now the idealism of youth is present in nations just as in individuals, though probably a nation is less conscious of it than an individual. It is with the nation one of the effects of the instinct of self-preservation, and for a youthful nation to absorb the vices of an old decadent one would be self-destruction. Thus the youthful Rome rejected most of the Etruscan poison, and thus nature purified herself, and Etruria was buried in the pit of her own nastiness.

There was however one town which acted as an interpreter between Rome and Etruria, and was the original cult-centre for a very great goddess, spreading her cult in both directions, into Rome and into Etruria. The town was Falerii and the goddess was Minerva, who in a certain sense entered Rome three times, once direct from Falerii to Rome, and once from Falerii to Rome by way of Etruria, and finally, when Falerii was captured by the Romans, again direct to Rome. In the earliest period there are scarcely any traces of the worship of Minerva in [Pg 45] Latium or Southern Italy, and we are absolutely certain that she was not known in Rome. In the country north of Rome, however, the situation is different There she is found quite frequently, especially in Etruria under the name of MENERVA or MENRVA. Yet she cannot have been an Etruscan goddess, because the name itself is Italic and not Etruscan. She is therefore neither Roman, nor Etruscan, nor Latin, at least so far as we know Latin in Latium. If we can find a place however where a Latin people is under strong Etruscan influence, we shall be near the solution. Such a place is Falerii, in the country of the Faliscans. To the ancients it appeared so thoroughly Etruscan that they go out of their way to explain that it was not. As a matter of fact it was the only Latin town on the right bank of the Tiber, and because of its locality it was early brought into vital connection with the Etruscans, so vital that while it never lost all of its original Latin character, it lost enough of it to exercise a very considerable direct influence over Etruria, and to be to a very large extent influenced by her in turn. We cannot of course positively prove that Minerva was originally worshipped only at Falerii, and that her cult spread entirely from this one point, but we have at least strong negative evidence, and so far as the general history of ancient religion is concerned there is nothing impossible in such a spread. Religious history [Pg 46] shows many parallels to this; for example the classic case of the god Eros of Thespiae, in Boeotia, who would have lived and died merely a little insignificant local god, if it had not been for the Boeotian poet Hesiod who adopted Eros into his poetry and thus gave him a start in life by which he ultimately succeeded in going all over the Greek world, and then passing into Rome as Cupid; and so into all later times.

We are accustomed to think of Minerva as the Latin name for Athena, the daughter of Zeus, and unconsciously we clothe Minerva with all the glory of Athena and endow her with Athena's many-sidedness. In reality the little peasant goddess of Falerii had originally nothing in common with Athena except the fact that both of them were interested in handicraft and the handicraftsman, but Athena had a hundred other interests besides, while this one thing seems to have filled the whole of Minerva's horizon. When Minerva went on her travels into Etruria, she came among a people who eventually learned from the representations of Greek art a very considerable amount of Greek mythology, and who, when they heard of Athena, saw her resemblance to Minerva and began thus to associate the two. But even in this association Minerva was still pre-eminently the goddess of the artisan and the labouring man, she was the patroness of the works of man's hands rather than of the works of his mind, [Pg 47] and as such she was brought into Rome by Etruscan and Faliscan workmen. At first she was worshipped merely by these workmen in their own houses, but by degrees as the number of these workmen increased and as a knowledge of their handicraft spread to native Romans, Minerva became so prominent that the state was compelled to acknowledge her, and to accept her among the gods of the state. But it was a very different acknowledgment from that of Hercules or Castor; these gods had been received inside the *pomerium*, but Minerva was given a temple outside, over on the Aventine. None the less her cult throve, and her power was soon shown both religiously and socially. Her great festival was on the 19th of March, a day which had been originally sacred to Mars, but the presence of Minerva's celebrations on that day soon caused the associations with Mars to be almost entirely forgotten. Socially her temple became the meeting-place of all the artisans of Rome, it was at once their religious centre and their business headquarters. There they met in their primitive guilds (*collegia*) and arranged their affairs, and thus it continued to be as long as pagan Rome lasted. The respect shown to these guilds of Minerva is nowhere more clearly exhibited than in an incident which happened in the time of the Second Punic War, several centuries after the introduction of the cult. Terrified by adverse portents the Roman Senate instructed the old poet [Pg 48] Livius Andronicus to write a hymn in honour of Juno and to train a chorus of youths and maidens to sing it. The hymn was sung, and was such a great success that the gratitude of the Senate took the form of granting permission to the poets of the city to have a guild of their own, and a meeting-place along with the older guilds in the temple of Minerva on the Aventine. This was the Roman state's first expression of literary appreciation; from her standpoint it was flattery indeed, for were not poets by this decree made equal to butchers, bakers, and cloth-makers, and was not poetry acknowledged to be of some practical use and adjudged a legitimate occupation?

The history of the cult of Minerva is much more complicated than that of Hercules or Castor. Like them she was subjected to strong Greek influence, and, as we shall see later, not very long after her introduction she was taken into the company of Juppiter and Juno, thus forming the famous Capitoline triad. Also temples were built to her individually under various aspects of the worship of Athena with whom she gradually became identified, but in the old Aventine temple the original idea of Minerva, the working man's friend, continued practically unchanged. Doubtless the society of Servius's day, who witnessed the coming of Minerva, did not realise what this introduction meant, and how absolutely necessary it was for Rome's future develop [Pg 49] ment that the artisan class should be among her people, and that this class should be represented in the world of the gods. They little knew that in the temple on the Aventine was being brought to expression the trade-union idea, which was to pass over into the mediaeval guild of both workmen and masters, still under religious auspices, and to find a latter-day parody in the modern labour-union, with its spirit of hostility to employers, and its indifference, at least as an organisation, to things religious.

Trade and handicraft were thus added to the Roman world, of men on earth, and of the gods above the earth, and it remains for us to consider the awakening of the political spirit and its corresponding religious phenomenon; but before we do this, we must clear the way by casting aside one ancient hypothesis connected with Servius's religious reforms, which is not correct, at least in the way in which the ancients meant it.

The writing of the earlier period of Rome's history is sometimes complicated rather than helped by the statements of the generally well-meaning but often misguided historians of later times. Their real knowledge of the facts was in many cases no greater than ours, while they lacked what modern historians possess: a breadth of view and a knowledge of the phenomena of history in many periods and among many nations. The study of the social and religious movements under Servius presents us with [Pg 50] an interesting illustration of this. It was customary namely to ascribe to Servius Tullius the introduction of the cult of Fortuna, and Plutarch takes occasion twice in his *Moralia* to describe the interest of Servius in this cult and to recount the extraordinary number of temples which he built to the great goddess of chance under her various attributes. The Romans of Plutarch's day thought of Fortuna in very much the way in which their poets, especially Horace, described her, as a great and powerful goddess of chance, the personification of the element of apparent caprice which seems to be present in the running of the universe. It is very much our way of thinking of her, and of course both our own concept and the later Roman concept go back to Greece. But Greece had not always had this idea of the goddess of luck. The older purer age of Greek thought was permeated with the idea of the absolute immutable character of the divine will, a belief which precluded the possibility of chance or caprice. The earliest Greek Tyche (Fortuna) was the daughter of Zeus who fulfilled his will; and that his will through her was often a beneficent will is shown in the tendency to think of her as a goddess of plenty. It was only the growth of scepticism, the failure of faith to bear up under the apparently contradictory lessons of experience, which brought into being in the Alexandrian age Tyche, the goddess of chance, the winged capricious deity [Pg 51] poised on the ball. It was this habit of thought which eventually gave the Romans that idea of Fortuna which has becamc our idea because it is the prevalent one in Roman literature and life in the periods with which we are most familiar. Now if Fortuna be thought of in this latter way, it is a very easy matter to connect her with Servius Tullius, for the legendary accounts of Servius's career picture him as a very child of "fortune," raised from the lowest estate to the highest power, the little slave boy who became king. What goddess would he delight to honour, if not the goddess of the happy chance which had made him what he was?

All this is very pretty, but it is unfortunately quite impossible, because whatever the time may have been when Fortuna began to be worshipped in Rome, it is certain that the idea of chance did not enter into the concept of her until long after Servius's day. Instead the early Fortuna was a goddess of plenty and fertility, among mankind as a protectress of women and of childbirth, among the crops and the herds as a goddess of fertility and fecundity. Her full name was probably Fors Fortuna, a name which survived in two old temples across the river from Rome proper, in Trastevere, where she was worshipped in the country by the farmers in behalf of the crops. Fortuna is thus merely the cult-name added to the old goddess Fors to intensify her meaning, which finally broke off from her and [Pg 52] became independent, expressing the same idea of a goddess of plenty. Later under Greek influence the concept of luck, especially good-luck, slowly displaced the older idea. The possibility of such a transition from fertility to good-luck is shown us in the phrase "*arbor felix,*" which originally meant a fruitful tree and later a tree of good omen. As regards Fortuna and Servius therefore there is no inherent reason why they should have been connected, and whenever it was that Fortuna began to exist, be it before or after Servius, she came into the world as a goddess of plenty and did not turn into a goddess of luck till centuries after her birth.

It must not be supposed that Rome in this sixth century before Christ could take into herself all these traders and artisans, and become thus interested also among her own citizens in these new employments, without receiving a corresponding impulse toward a larger political life. Thus there began that ever-increasing participation in the affairs of the Latin league, which was her first step toward acquiring a world dominion. It is probable that Rome had always belonged to this league, but at first as a very insignificant member. Those were the days in which Alba Longa stood out as leader, a leadership which she afterwards lost, but of which the recollection was retained because the Alban Mount behind Alba Longa remained the cult-centre, connected with the worship of the god of the league, the Juppiter of the [Pg 53] Latins (Juppiter Latiaris), not only until B.C. 338 when the league ceased to exist, but even later when Rome kept up a sentimental celebration of the old festival. In the course of time, for reasons which we do not know, Alba Longa's power declined and the mantle of her supremacy fell upon Aricia, a little town still in existence not far from Albano. The coming of Aricia to the presidency of the league started a religious movement which is one of the most extraordinary in the checkered history of Roman religion. The ultimate result of this movement was the introduction of the goddess Diana into the state-cult of Rome, where she was subsequently identified with Apollo's sister Artemis. But this is a long story, and to understand it we must go back some distance to make our beginning.

Among the more savage tribes and in the wilder mountain regions of both Greece and Italy there was worshipped a goddess who had a different name in each country, Artemis in Greece, Diana in Italy, but who was in nature very much the same. This does not imply that it was the same goddess originally or that the early Artemis of Greece had any influence on the Diana of Italy. Their similarity was probably caused merely by the similarity of the conditions from which they sprang, the similar needs of the two peoples. She was a goddess of the woods, and of nature, and especially of wild animals, a patroness of the hunt and the huntsman, but also a goddess of all [Pg 54] small animals, of all helpless little ones, and a helper too of those that bore them, hence a goddess of birth, and in the sphere of mankind a goddess of women and of childbirth. Later in Greece Artemis was absorbed into the sea-cult of Apollo on the island of Delos, where she became Apollo's sister, like him the child of Latona; but naturally Diana experienced no similar change until in Rome, centuries later, she was artificially identified with Artemis. In the earliest times there were two places in Italy where the cult of Diana was especially prominent, both, as we should expect, in wooded mountainous regions: one on Mount Tifata (near Capua), the modern St. Angelo in Formis; the other in Latium, in a grove near Aricia. It is with this latter cult-centre that we have here to do. The grove near Aricia became so famous that the goddess worshipped there was known as "Diana of the Grove" (Diana Nemorensis), and the place where she was worshipped was called the

"Grove" (*nemus*), a name which is still retained in the modern "Nemi." She was a goddess of the woods, of the animal kingdom, of birth, and so of women; and almost all the dedicatory inscriptions which have been found near her shrine were put up by women. She was worshipped above all by the people of Aricia, and she seems to have been the patron deity of the town. When it fell to Aricia's lot to become the head of the league, her goddess Diana promptly assumed an important position in the league, not [Pg 55] because she had by nature any political bearing whatsoever, but merely because she was wedded to Aricia, and experienced all the vicissitudes of her career. Thus there came into the league, alongside of the old Juppiter Latiaris of the Alban Mount, the new Diana Nemorensis of Aricia, and sacrifices to her formed a part of the solemn ritual of the united towns of Latium. It does not take actually a great many years for a religious custom to acquire sanctity, and before many generations had passed, Diana was felt to be quite as original and essential a part of the worship of the league as Juppiter himself. During these same centuries Rome was growing in importance and influence in the league, until, instead of being one of its insignificant towns, she was in a fair way to become its president. Here her diplomacy stepped in to help her. The league was of course essentially a political institution, but in a primitive society political institutions are still in tutelage to religious ones, and the direct road to strong political influence lies through religious zeal. The way to leadership in the Latin league lay through excessive devotion to Juppiter and Diana. It is therefore no accidental coincidence that we find Rome in the period of Servius building a temple to Juppiter Latiaris on the top of the Alban Mount, and introducing the worship of Diana into Rome, building her a temple on the Aventine, hence outside the *pomerium*. Yet it was not the introduction of her worship as an [Pg 56] ordinary state-cult, for then she would have been taken inside the *pomerium* with far greater right than Hercules and Castor were. It was, on the contrary, the building of a sanctuary of the league outside the *pomerium*, yet inside the civil wall; not the adoption of Diana as a Roman goddess, but the close association of the Diana of the Latin league with Rome. It was the attempt to put Rome religiously as well as politically into the position which Aricia held; and it was successful. Diana was still the league-goddess; tradition has it that the league helped to build the temple; and the dedication day of the temple, August 13, was the same as that of the temple at Nemi. The Roman temple was outside the *pomerium* therefore, not because she was a foreign goddess like Minerva, but because as a league-goddess she must be outside, not inside, the sacred wall of Rome.

Diana had been introduced for a specific purpose as part of a diplomatic game, not because Rome felt any real religious need of her; it is hardly to be expected therefore that her subsequent career in Rome would be of any great importance. Naturally when once the state had taken the responsibility of the cult upon itself, that cult was assured as long as pagan Rome lasted, for the state was always faithful, at least in the mechanical performance of a ritual act; but popular interest could not be counted on, especially as many of the things which Diana stood [Pg 57] for, for example her relation to women, were ably represented by Juno. It is not likely that Diana would ever have been of importance in the religion of subsequent time, had it not been for another accident which served to keep alive the interest in Diana, just as the accident of Diana's connection with the Latin league had aroused that interest in the beginning. This was the coming of Apollo and his sister Artemis. Apollo came first, probably during the time of Servius, but Artemis seems to have come much later, not before B.C. 431. Her identification with Diana was inevitable, and from that time onward Diana begins a new life with all the attributes and myths of Artemis, but this new Artemis-Diana was quite as different a goddess from the old Aventine Diana as the new Athena-Minerva was from the old Aventine Minerva.

The political interest of the Romans had been aroused, they had found their life-work, their career was opening before them, and it must not be supposed that the reflex action of this new political spirit on the religious world was confined to the building of two league temples, one to Juppiter Latiaris on the Alban Mount, miles away from Rome, and one to Diana outside the *pomerium* over in the woods of the Aventine. This political interest was no artificial acquisition, but the inevitable expression of an instinct. It must therefore find its representation inside the city, in connexion [Pg 58] with a deity who was already deep in the hearts of the people. This deity could be none other than the sky-father Juppiter, who had stood by them in the old days of their exclusively farming life, sending them sunshine and rain in due season. Up on the Capitoline he was worshipped as *Feretrius*, "the striker," in his most fearful attribute as the god of the lightning. To him the richest spoils of war (*spolia opima*) were due, and to him the conqueror gave thanks on his return from battle. It was this Juppiter of the Capitoline who was chosen to be the divine representative of Rome's political ambition; and her confidence in the future, and the omen of her inevitable success lay in the cult-names, the *cognomina*, with which this Juppiter was henceforth and forever adorned, Juppiter Optimus Maximus. These adjectives are no mere idle ornament, no purely pleasant phraseology; they express not merely the excellence of Rome's Juppiter but his absolute superiority to all other Juppiters, including Juppiter Latiaris. And so while Rome with one hand was building a temple for the league on the Alban Mount, merely as a member of the league, with the other hand she was building a temple in the heart of her city to a god who was to bring into subjection to himself all other gods who dared to challenge his supremacy, just as the city which paid him honour was to overcome all other cities which refused to acknowledge her. From henceforth Juppiter Optimus [Pg 59] Maximus represents all that is most truly Roman in Rome. It was under his banner that her battles were fought, it was to him in all time to come that returning generals gave thanks.

Tradition sets the completion of the Capitoline temple in the first year of the republic, but the idea and the actual beginning of the work belong to the later kingdom and hence to our present period, and the contemplation of it forms a fitting close to the development which we have tried to sketch. And now that this part of our work is over it may be well to ask ourselves what we have seen, for there have been so many bypaths which we have of necessity explored, that the main road we have travelled may not be entirely distinct in our mind. In the period which corresponds to the later kingdom, and roughly to the sixth century before Christ, and which we have called "Servian" for convenience, we have watched a primitive pastoral community, isolated from the world's life, turning into a small city-state with political interests, the beginnings of trade and handicraft, and various rival social classes; and we have seen how along with the coming of these outside interests there came various new cults connected with them, most of them implying entirely new deities, and only one or two of them new sides of old deities. The body of old Roman religion had received its first blows; what Tacitus (*Hist.* i. 4) says of the downfall of the empire—"Then was that [Pg 60] secret of the empire disclosed, that it was possible for a ruler to be appointed elsewhere than at Rome"—is true of Roman religion in this period when it was discovered that the state might take into itself deities from outside Rome. And yet while the principle itself was fatal, the practice of it, so far, had been without much harm. Rome's growth was inevitable, it was quite as inevitable that these new interests should be represented in the world of the gods; her old gods did not suffice, hence new ones were introduced. But the actual gods brought in thus far were harmless; Hercules, Castor, Minerva, Diana never did Rome any injury in themselves, never injured her national *morale*, never lowered the tone of earnest sobriety which had been characteristic of the old regime.

So far it was good, and well had it been for Rome if she could have shut the gate of her Olympus now. What the old religion had not provided was now present. Politics, trade, and art were now represented. With these she was abundantly supplied for all her future career. But that was not to be, the gate was still open, and the destructive influence of Greece was soon to send in a host of new deities, who were destined not only to overwhelm the old Roman gods—which in itself we might forgive—but to sap away the old Roman virtues, to the maintenance of which the atmosphere of these old gods was essential. The forerunner of [Pg 61] this influence was in himself innocent enough, it was Apollo, and it is to his coming and the subsequent developments which set him in distinct opposition to Juppiter Optimus Maximus that we now turn.

[Pg 62]

THE COMING OF THE SIBYL

The Rome of the first consuls was a very different Rome from that of the earlier kings. Not only was the population larger but it was divided socially into different classes. The simple patriarchal one-class community had been transformed into the complex structure of a society which had in it virtually all those elements and interests, except the more strictly intellectual ones, which go to make up what we call society in the modern sense. The world of the gods also had increased in population, and there too there was present a slight social distinction between the old gods (*Indigetes*) and the new-comers (*Novensides*), though it is open to question how strongly this distinction was felt. The new gods thus far were not incommensurable with the old ones. They formed a tolerably harmonious circle, and there was not felt to be any need of new priesthoods; the old priests were sufficient to look after them all. There were a few new names, and a few new temples or altars, but everything was in the old spirit, and there [Pg 63] was no rivalry between the old and the new. None of the old gods was crowded into the background by the new-comers. This was on the face of it impossible as yet, because the new gods all represented new ideas which had not been provided for under the old scheme. Even Diana, who afterwards usurped somewhat the functions of Juno, stood at present preeminently for the political idea pure and simple, so far as Rome was concerned. This period of equipoise did not continue very long, but while it lasted it was beyond doubt the best and strongest period in the whole history of Roman religion. There was no violent religious enthusiasm, but then there was no corresponding depression offsetting it. It was the cold but conscientious formalism which was best adapted to the Roman character, because so long as it held sway the excesses of superstition were avoided.

But this element of superstition was already on the way, it came in within a few years of the opening of the republic, and it exercised its insidious influence ever more and more powerfully until it celebrated its wildest orgies in the time of the Second Punic War. It is in this period of the first three centuries of the republic, roughly from B.C. 500 to B.C. 200, that this change was produced. Outwardly it resembled a steady growth in religious feeling and enthusiasm, and it might well have seemed so to contemporaries. It was a period of many new gods [Pg 64] and many new temples, but this in itself was no harm. It was the principle behind it which did the damage. It was the essential contradiction to what true Roman religion and Roman character demanded; and the last half of the republic paid the price for what the first half had done, in a decline of faith which has scarcely been exceeded in the world's history.

It has been customary for writers on the history of Roman morals to attribute these changes to the coming of Greek influence; and of course in the main this is correct, but these writers have in general neglected to analyse this Greek influence more closely, and to distinguish the various aspects of it in different periods, and to ask and answer the question why this influence should be so particularly harmful to the Romans. It is generally spoken of as the influence of Greek literature and philosophy, but for our present period this is entirely incorrect, for we all know that Greek literature did not begin to influence Rome until the time of the Punic wars, and yet the Greek influence of which we speak here began to exert its effects two hundred and fifty years before the Punic wars. The real cause of the unnatural stimulation of religion during these three centuries is nothing more nor less than the books of the Sibylline oracles. It is therefore a very definite and interesting problem which we have before us. It is to examine the [Pg 65] workings of these oracles and to explain why they had such an extraordinary effect on religion and society, that in three centuries they could entirely change both the form and the content of Roman religion, and under the guise of increasing its zeal, so sap its vitality that it required almost two hundred years of human experience and suffering before true religion was in some sense at least restored to its own place.

Like the origin of almost all the great religious movements in the world's history, the beginnings of the Sibylline books are shrouded in mystery. A later age, for whom history had no secrets, with a cheap would-be omniscience told of the old woman who visited Tarquin and offered him nine books for a certain price, and when he refused to pay it, went away, burned three, and then returning offered him at the original price the six that were left; on his again refusing she went away, burned three more and finally offered at the same old price the three that remained, which he accepted. Except as a sidelight on the character of the early Greek trader the story is worthless. It is doubtful even if the presence of the Sibylline books in Rome goes back beyond the republic. The first dateable use of them was in the year B.C. 496, and there is one little fact connected with them which makes it probable that they did not come in until the republic had begun. This is the circumstance that in view [Pg 66] of the great secrecy of the books it is unthinkable that they should ever have been in Rome without especial guardians, and yet the earliest guardians that we know of were a newly made priesthood consisting originally of two men, the so-called "two men in charge of the sacrifices" (*IIviri sacris faciundis*). Now the form of this title is peculiar; it is not a proper name like the titles of all the other priesthoods. Instead it is built on the plan of the titles of the special committees appointed by the Senate for administrative purposes; it bears every mark therefore of having arisen under the republic, rather than under the kingdom, at a time when the Senate had the supreme control. So much may be said regarding the time when they were introduced into Rome; as for the place from which they came, this was without doubt the Greek colonies of Southern Italy, probably the oldest and most important of them, Cumae, so famous for its Sibyl. This was not the first association that Rome had had with Cumae, for in all probability the worship of Apollo had spread from there into Rome toward the close of the kingdom. Apollo and the books were connected at Cumae, for it was Apollo who inspired the Sibyl, and the oracles were his commands, but it is almost certain that Apollo came to Rome in advance of the oracles. He came there as a god of healing and was given a sacred place outside the *pomerium* in the Campus Martius, on the spot [Pg 67] where later (B.C. 431) a temple was built for him with his sister Artemis-Diana and their mother Latona. This was the only state temple that Apollo ever had, until Augustus built the famous one on the Palatine. It was in the wake of Apollo that the Sibylline books came. As for the books themselves, they were kept so secret that we cannot expect to know much about them, but in rare cases where the seriousness of the exigency warranted it, the Senate permitted the actual publication of the oracle upon which its action was based, and of the oracles thus published one or two have been preserved to us. They were of course written in Greek and were phrased in the ambiguous style which for obvious reasons was the most advantageous style for oracles. They commanded the worship of certain specific deities, naturally all of them Greek, and the performance of certain more or less complicated ritual acts. When they were received in Rome, they were placed in the temple of Juppiter Optimus Maximus on the Capitoline in the keeping of their guardians, the new priesthood of the "two men in charge of the sacrifices." This committee of two was enlarged to ten in B.C. 367 when the great compromise between the

Patricians and the Plebeians was made, and the Plebeians were admitted into this one priesthood, with five representatives. Subsequently Sulla made the number fifteen, which continued as the official number from [Pg 68] that time on, so that the priesthood is ordinarily called the *Quindecemviri*, even when one of the older periods is referred to. The real control of the books however lay in the hands of the Senate. When the Senate saw fit, the priests were ordered to consult the books, but without this special command even their guardians dared not approach them. The priests reported to the Senate what they had found, and the Senate then decreed whatever actions the oracles commanded. The carrying out of these actions was again in the charge of the Sibylline priests, who performed the ceremonies demanded and were for all time to come responsible for the maintenance of any new cults which might be introduced.

When we see how carefully these oracles were guarded and how circumspectly their use was hedged about by senatorial control, and when we think how relatively little harm the use of oracles had wrought in Greece in all the centuries of her history, it may well seem as if the statements made in the beginning of this chapter about the havoc caused by these oracles were grossly exaggerated. But the efforts of the Senate to safeguard these oracles only prove that the older and wiser men in the community realised how dangerous they were, and the comparison with Greece leads to a consideration of certain essential differences between the Greek and the Roman temperament which made that which was meat for one into poison for the other. [Pg 69]

In the older purer age of Greece the gods were never far away from men, they lived almost side by side with them; there were to be sure many gods of whom they were afraid and from whom they desired to keep as far away as possible, but there were a great many other gods of whom they liked to think. In constructing the records of their history they did not work backwards from the light of the present into an ever darkening past, but they began from the beginning in the full light of the gods from whom all things sprang, and mythology passed into history by imperceptible gradations. They knew more about the beginning when all things were completely in the hands of the gods than they did about their immediate past. Art began very early to make them familiar with the appearance of the gods, so that there was little that was mysterious about their religion, so little that the element of mystery had later to be almost artificially cultivated in the "mysteries." They respected the gods rather than feared them, and they felt that the gods would do them no harm unless they themselves first sinned against them or their own fellow-men, and the oracles of Delphi were no more terrifying to them than the coming of the word of God was to the prophets of Israel. They were accustomed to these messages, which were almost every-day affairs. It was all a part of that marvellous poise of nature which made the every-day mortal Greek almost as [Pg 70] calm as the unperturbed imperturbable faces of their gods as their great sculptors saw them.

In Rome all was very different. The superstitious element in the Italian character, which amazes us so much to-day when cultured twentieth century men and women in good society persecute their fellows because of the evil eye, is a heritage of many thousand years. Sometimes it seems as if it were the Italian birthright, the blight of Etruria which came into their nature in spite of themselves. It required centuries to educate the Roman into the concept of personal individual gods. He had begun his theological career by terror of unknown powers all about him, and by regarding religion as the science of propitiating the right power on the right occasion. One could not know these powers, one did not desire to. Their gods were at once their masters and their servants, but never their companions. The early Roman knew no such thing as an oracle, the only messages from the gods were the expressions of their wrath, in the sending of prodigies and portents. They did indeed consult the gods by watching the flight of birds or studying the entrails of the sacrifice, but it was merely to obtain a "yes or no" answer to a categorical question as to whether a certain act was pleasing to the gods. Otherwise all about them lay mystery, and at the point where sight failed, since neither imagination nor faith carried them any further, superstition [Pg 71] stepped in, and the more they thought of the gods the more terrified they became. Now if you present to a people thus constituted a divine book of infallible oracles, you increase their terror in greater measure than the book itself can assuage it, and with the use of the book the simpler forms of their old belief will grow less and less effective in the face of this new "witchcraft," which can work wonders. And no matter how you may hedge the use of the book about, it will be used more and more as the craving for magic is increasingly aroused.

The study of the outward and the inward effects of the Sibylline books is therefore the real history of religion in the first half of the republic. The outward effects are seen in the introduction of a series of Greek gods, who were in themselves in the main eminently respectable, and whose presence was in itself no offence to good morals, and if we stop there we fail to understand why the religious interest of the Second Punic War should change so quickly to the scepticism of the following century. The inward effects however, which, though they are hard to see, may yet be discovered between the lines of the chronicle, will explain all the undermining of foundation, until we wonder not why the structure collapsed so suddenly but how it managed to last so long.

The history of the activity of the books begins peaceably enough. In the year B.C. 496 Rome was [Pg 72] in a bad way; her crops had failed and the importation of grain from Latium was rendered very difficult because of the war with the Latins in which she was engaged. In her distress she turned to the Sibylline books, and on the occasion of this their first recorded use, the oracles ordered the introduction into Rome of the cult of three Greek deities, Demeter, Dionysos, and Kore. It was a most appropriate and characteristic choice. In the first place the deities in question were worshipped at Cumae, the home of the books, whence Rome could, and probably did, borrow the cult; and in the second place Demeter was the goddess of grain, and it was from Cumae that Rome was already beginning to obtain her imported grain supply. Thus the coming of the Cumaean Demeter into the religious world of Rome is but the sacred parallel to the coming of Cumaean grain into the material world of Rome. The Greek goddess of grain came with the grain, just as Castor had come with the Greek cavalry, with this essential distinction however that Demeter came by the incantation of the books and the enactment of the Senate, whereas Castor's coming was a slow and normal development.

It is important to notice closely exactly what happened when these deities were introduced, partly because they form the first recorded instance, and hence may well have acted as a model for subsequent repetitions of the act, but also because we have a more definite knowledge of the phenomena in this [Pg 73] case than in many others. In the first place it is clear that the deities were felt to be foreign: not only was their temple built out the Aventine way, in the valley of the Circus Maximus, outside the *pomerium*, but—a much more significant fact—their Greek names were dropped, and they were given Roman names instead, to make them seem less out of place. Then too these Roman names were not new names, translations of their Greek titles, but were the names of already existing Roman deities with whom they were easily identified, so that we see at once that their coming was no real enrichment of the Roman Olympus; what they stood for was already represented there, and their coming was simply a reduplication, with the consequent result that as these parvenus increased in prominence and influence, they robbed of all their vitality the sober old Roman deities to whom they had attached themselves. What were these original deities who were thus doomed to death in B.C. 496? Demeter took the name of the old Roman goddess Ceres, a goddess of fertility, about whom we know just enough to assert that she belonged to the old religion of Numa and that she was at heart quite a different person from Demeter. All the rest is lost, submerged under the new Demeter-Ceres with her temple built by Greek architects and her April games. It is this new Ceres who soon develops an extraordinary political importance because her temple is to the [Pg 74] Plebeians as a class what the temple of Minerva is to the unions of organised labour. It is there that they have their meeting-place, and the temple itself is always their treasury as contrasted with the Saturn temple, the treasury of the state as a whole. The very officers of the Plebeians, the famous Plebeian aediles, get their name from association with this temple (*aedes*). This political side of her activity is the only real advantage, except the grain itself, connected with her importation; the two form at best a poor economic compensation for the ever increasing immoral effects of the public games of Ceres.

But though Ceres is the most important of the three deities economically and politically, we must not forget the other two, both of whom are interesting, though one of them more for what she is not than for what she is. Along with Demeter came Dionysos and Demeter's daughter Kore: the three were associated in the solemn mysteries of Eleusis, but none of the beauty of these ideas went over into the Roman cult. Demeter was merely the deified grain-traffic, and Dionysos was little else than the god of wine, while poor Kore fell out without any particular content for a curious reason that we shall see in a moment. The only old Roman deity with whom Dionysos could be identified was the god Liber, who had had a rather interesting history, and who had done enough along the line of self-develop [Pg 75] ment to deserve a better fate than to be crushed to insignificance under the prominence of his new namesake. Liber was at this time a flourishing god of fertility and, since the introduction of the grape into Italy, especially the patron of the fruit of the vine, but he had made his own career, and there was a time when he had no individuality of his own but was merely a cult-adjective of the great god Juppiter, the giver of all fertility in every phase of life. Thus out of the original Juppiter-Liber there had grown the independent god Liber; and now this Liber lost his individuality by identification with Dionysos. Finally comes Kore, Demeter's daughter. Here the Romans were hard put to it to find a goddess who represented any similar content, and after all this was no light task because Kore has little meaning unless she is taken also as Persephone, Pluto's bride—a process which required a mythological knowledge and appreciation in which the Romans of the early republic were totally lacking. But there was an old goddess Libera, a shadowy potentiality contrasted and paired with the masculine Liber, and they chose her and gave Kore her name. We have a curious proof of how little the Romans knew of Kore-Libera, and of how purely mechanical both the introduction of Kore and her identification with Libera were, in the fact that about two hundred and fifty years later, as we shall see, Persephone, the real Kore, was introduced into Rome as an [Pg 76] altogether new deity, and existed there side by side with Libera for at least a century before people began to realise that Proserpina and Libera stood for the same Greek goddess.

It was necessary to go into these details in order that we might understand as much as possible of the process by which the gods of the Sibylline books were assimilated into the body of Roman religion. We see how in the main they were superfluous and therefore unnecessary and even undesirable because by their presence they robbed old Roman deities of their existence, and how those elements in them which were least in accord with the old Roman spirit were most apt to develop, and how in general their adoption was a purely mechanical process, like any act in witchcraft, where the form is all important because the meaning cannot be understood, and how totally different therefore the estate of these gods was in Rome from what it had been in Greece, because in Rome they were introduced, stripped of all their mythology, worshipped only for their practical bearings, and compelled therefore to work for their living.

The importation of grain from Cumae meant more to Rome than the mere satisfaction of her physical needs; it meant much more than the addition of three deities to her state-cult, for the grain thus imported was carried from Cumae to Ostia by sea and so up the Tiber to Rome, and the [Pg 77] whole matter therefore marks one of the important steps in Rome's interest in commerce generally but especially in ocean commerce. As yet she did not do the actual carrying herself, but she began to be interested in it, and the sea began to mean something to this inland town. This increased interest in trade in general and this inceptive interest in those who "go down to the sea in ships" have both of them left their reflexion in the religious life of the time; two new deities are introduced, both of them almost certainly by means of the Sibylline oracles, though some accidental blanks in our historical tradition have deprived us of details.

The chronicle of the year B.C. 495 tells us that there was a dispute in that year as to who should dedicate the temple of Mercury. This is Mercury's first appearance in our sources. The circumstances of the vowing of the temple have been omitted through some oversight, but in spite of this the connexion of his introduction with the Sibylline books is beyond all reasonable doubt, for the simple reason that the guardians of the oracles always looked after his cult in all subsequent time. Notwithstanding the suddenness of his appearance and the silence of the chronicle, his story is quite clear and his past history easy to restore, at least in outline.

The versatile Hermes, who as messenger of the gods plays a part in so many Greek myths, became in the course of time among other things associated [Pg 78] with travelling, as god of roads, and also with trade, partly because trading necessitates travelling, and partly because Hermes was also the protector of the market-place in which the trading was done. Thus he was called "Hermes Protector of the Merchant" (*Empolaios*) and in this capacity went into the colonies of Greece, including those of Southern Italy. Thus Hermes travelled with the grain merchant from Cumae and became known to the Romans. They however knew him merely as the god of trade, and their name for him is nothing but the translation into Latin of his Greek cult-title: *Empolaios* = *Mercurius*. For a long time it was thought that there had existed a Mercurius among the original gods of Rome, but the traces of this old god are apparent rather than real and suggest one phase of that pastime of which the later Romans were so fond, that of writing history backwards and putting an artificial halo of antiquity about the gods whom they borrowed from Greece. Thus Mercury was received into the state-cult at about the time when the grain trade began, and was, as it were, the divine representative of the interest which the Roman state took in the whole transaction. His temple was outside the *pomerium* on the Aventine side of the Circus Maximus. It was in this temple of the merchant god that the primitive Chamber of Commerce (*collegium mercatorum*) had its beginning, an association, partly sacral, partly commercial, whose members, the *mercuriales*, are [Pg 79] frequently met with in literature and also in inscriptions, one of which has been found as far away as the island of Delos. In the actual cult of the Romans Mercury never regained the many-sidedness which he had lost in coming to them merely as a god of trade. In this capacity he appears on the sextans of the old copper coinage, and under the empire he went into the provinces as the companion of Mars, since the merchant went side by side with the soldier. On the contrary when in the third century before Christ Greek literature came to Rome, this simple idea of Mercury was reinforced by many new Greek ideas and he entered into Roman poetry with all the attributes and functions of Hermes; but this had little or no effect on the cult and there were no great rivals to the old temple near the Circus Maximus, no cult-centre with advanced Greek ideas, as we have seen spring up in the case of Hercules, Castor, Minerva, and Diana.

We have already seen how the rise of the grain trade brought four new deities to Rome, but there is one more chapter to our story. The grain itself and the trade itself had now obtained their divine complements, but the sea had not yet received its due; it too must have its parallel among the gods of Rome. And so it came to pass that again under the influence of the fateful books, though exactly when or how we cannot say, the Greek Poseidon came into Rome. The sea had always meant much [Pg 80] to the Greeks, and the joyful shout of Xenophon's troops "The sea! the sea!" finds an echo all through the centuries of Greek history before and after the Anabasis. But the multitude of islands and harbours in Greece is in marked contrast to the dearth of them in Italy, where even to-day there is no good port of call on the west coast between Naples and Civitavecchia—and the latter would be useless, were it not for Trajan's mole. In Italy accordingly the sea-god Poseidon was worshipped only in the Greek colonies, where however he had two famous cults, one at Tarentum, later called Colonia Neptunia, and one at Paestum, whose old name was Poseidonia. The Romans had worshipped deities of water in abundance, as became an agricultural people, for water meant life, and drought, death; but their deities were those of the sweet waters of springs and rivers, they knew no god of the sea. But when the oracles brought Poseidon to Rome he was identified with an old Roman water-god Neptune, whose cult henceforward included the sea. We do not know where the shrine of the old sweet-water Neptune had been, but his old festival had occurred on July 23. The new Poseidon-Neptune was given a temple outside the *pomerium* in the Campus Martius, but the new was connected with the old in so far at least that the dedication day of the new temple was July 23, the day of the old Neptune festival.

With the introduction of Neptune, the sea-god, [Pg 81] the state had accomplished, as it were, a sort of divine marine insurance; the transport of the grain was now watched over by a Roman god; but it was not to be expected that the cult of a sea-god would ever mean very much to the Romans. The maritime commerce of the Eternal City was very slow in developing, and it grew to its subsequent proportions, not because the Romans of Italy engaged in it, but because those foreigners who took to the sea by nature later became Romans. Nor did naval warfare fall to her lot until the First Punic

War, and even then her victories were gained by the tactics of land fighting transferred to the decks of two ships, her own and the enemy's, fastened together by landing-bridges, and the glory of victory was due not to Neptune but to Mars. It was not until the civil wars at the close of the republic that real naval battles occurred, and that Neptune received his share of glory for the victory at Actium in B.C. 31, and later over Sextus Pompeius, in a temple erected by Agrippa in the Campus Martius, behind the beautiful columns of which the Roman Stock-Exchange transacts its business to-day.

In the first decade of the republic therefore, as we have seen, a group of Greek gods was introduced by the Sibylline oracles, no one of whom can be said to have been really needed, no one of whom except the sea-element in Neptune represented any new and vital principles not already present in the [Pg 82] religious world, if not of Numa, at least of Servius. The best that can be said of these gods is that one or two of them, notably Mercury and Neptune, exerted no positively detrimental influences on later generations. For the next two centuries our chronicles are silent, so far as the actual introduction of new deities by the aid of the books is concerned, and it is not until B.C. 293 that the narrative of new gods begins again. But in other ways the oracles were not idle during these two hundred years. We must rid ourselves of the idea that it was necessary that their consultation should always result in the importation of some new Greek deity. The oracles might order the carrying out of some new religious rite regarding the deities already present, and these religious rites, especially the public processions so frequently performed, feed the ever-growing superstition of the populace. It is essential to a charm or incantation that it should contain something strange or foreign, it is above all things help from without; and when the gods send prodigies and portents, when their statues weep and sweat blood, when cattle speak, and meteors fall from the sky, something strange and unusual must be done to counteract these things. Among the foreign acts thus ordered the sacred procession occurs frequently. It started from the temple of Apollo in the Campus Martius and passed into the city through the Porta Carmentalis, went across the Forum and then outside [Pg 83] the *pomerium* again to the temple of Ceres, and then to the temple of Juno Regina on the Aventine. It was therefore a power from without which came into their city to purify them and to carry away out of the city again the impurities of which it had rid the community.

It is also characteristic of such semi-magical things that they lose their effects after a few applications, and other things must be sought always more complicated and more strange. Thus from the beginning of the republic down through the Second Punic War we have a series of extraordinary measures, growing more and more complicated until in the religious frenzy of the years after Cannae even human sacrifices are performed at the command of the books. In this the third century before Christ deities begin again to be introduced, and it is to this century that we now turn.

It is probable that the Romans had always worshipped certain powers of healing, but what their names were under the old regime we do not know, except that possibly they were connected with the gods of water. At the close of the kingdom they received, as we have seen, Apollo the divine healer, Apollo Medicus, and this was originally the only side of his activity which he exercised at Rome. At various seasons of plague during the early centuries of the republic they called on him for help, and on one such occasion (B.C. 431) they built him [Pg 84] a temple. But in the course of time men began to think lightly of the old family physician who had stood by the Romans during more than two centuries; his methods were too conservative, they were felt not to be thoroughly up to date. A new god of healing had appeared in Rome, the Greek god Asklepios, whom myth called Apollo's son, though originally he had had no connection with Apollo. His great sanctuary was at Epidauros, and from there his cult spread over all the Greek world. At first he was known at Rome only in the worship of private individuals, who had brought him up from the Greek colonies of Southern Italy, probably Tarentum or Metapontum; but his cult was contagious, and the stories of his miraculous cures were eagerly heard. It is no wonder then that in the presence of a great pestilence in B.C. 293, when the Sibylline books were consulted, "it was found in the books," as Livy says, "that Aesculapius must be brought to Rome from Epidauros." The war with Pyrrhus however was on, and nothing could be done that year except the setting apart of a solemn day of prayer and supplication to Aesculapius. It is interesting to observe how much the Romans have changed since the time exactly two centuries before (B.C. 493), when Ceres and her companions, the first gods introduced by the books, received their temple. That was the acknowledgment of gods well known at Rome, and even then they were [Pg 85] immediately identified with already existing Roman gods; now they actually send an expedition not only outside of Rome but of Italy itself to bring in the cult of a god whom they accept by his Greek name. In the following year (B.C. 292) the expedition started for Epidauros to bring back the god, that is the sacred snake which was both his symbol and his visible presence. Such an importation of a sacred snake from Epidauros is not unique in the case of Rome, but was the normal method of establishing a branch cult. Snakes were kept at Epidauros for just this purpose, and many branches were thus established. It is an extremely interesting question as to the practical medical value of the methods of healing practised at Epidauros and its branches. For a long time those best fitted to express a technical opinion, modern physicians who examined the matter, found nothing good in them, and their opinion seems to receive confirmation from some of the inscriptions recently discovered at Epidauros, which tell the most extraordinary tales of miraculous cures. And yet many of these tales are not intended as actual facts, but rather as pious legends, proclaimed for the edification of the devout, in order that their faith might be quickened. Before we condemn the whole affair, we must realise two facts; one is that some of the most able minds of Greece, men who were otherwise by no means remarkable for their religious faith, believed implicitly in Epidauros and [Pg 86] went there to be cured; and the other is that the miraculous action of the god was always supplemented by medicines, in which there may well have been some real value.

We are told too much rather than too little about this embassy to Epidauros, for the atmosphere of this third century is different from that of the early republic. Greek literature was beginning to influence Rome, and those generations were being born who were to be the pioneers in Roman literature. Thus Roman mythology was commencing along Greek lines and with Greek models, and one of the points where legend grew thickest and fastest is in this coming of Aesculapius. The plain facts are evidently that the committee went to Epidauros, obtained the snake, brought it back safely to

Rome, and established the sanctuary on the island in the Tiber, where a temple was built and dedicated January 1, B.C. 291. Probably this was the first use to which the island had ever been put, and from this time dates the first bridge connecting it with the city; the other bridge, to the right bank, was much later. The Romans had always considered the island a disadvantage rather than an advantage. Even in legend it was cursed, for it sprang from the wheat of the Tarquins. They had always desired to be cut off from it, and had always feared lest it might act as a means of approach for the enemy from the opposite bank. The few real facts of [Pg 87] Aesculapius's coming grew into a romantic account of how, to the great surprise and terror of the sailors, the snake went of its own accord into the Roman ship; and how it stayed aboard until they reached Antium, and then suddenly swam ashore and coiled itself up in a sacred palm tree in the enclosure of the temple of Apollo there; and how, when they were in despair of ever getting it back again, it returned peaceably to them at the end of three days, and all went well on the journey to Ostia and up the Tiber until they were passing the island, when the snake went ashore to make its permanent home there.

It was a pretty fancy which at a later date formed the island into the likeness of a boat by building a prow and stem of travertine at either end, the traces of which may still be seen; and it is a curious instance of the many survivals of ancient Rome in the modern city, that the Hospital of S. Bartolommeo stands on the site of the old Aesculapius sanctuary, and so far as we can tell, twenty-two centuries of suffering humanity have had the burden of their pain lightened there, in uninterrupted succession since that new year's day, above three hundred years before Christ, when the hospital of Aesculapius of Epidauros was formally opened.

The coming of the god of healing in the opening years of the third century may well be regarded as [Pg 88] an omen of the great suffering which that century was to bring to Rome. It was a century of almost uninterrupted warfare: first the Samnite war; then the war with Pyrrhus and Rome's conquest of Southern Italy; then after a breathing spell of about a decade the first war with Carthage, and Rome's bitter apprenticeship in fighting at sea; then campaigns in Cisalpine Gaul; and finally the war with Hannibal roughly filling the last two decades, the most fearful contest in all Rome's history, with her most terrible enemy in her own land of Italy. It is little to be wondered at therefore that this was in the main a century of religious depression, a time when the fear of the gods filled every man's heart and when every trifling apparent irregularity in the course of nature was exaggerated into a portent declaring the wrath of the gods and needing some immediate and extraordinary propitiation. It is in just such a moment as this in the middle of the century (B.C. 249) that the next recorded instance of new gods occurs. The first war with Carthage was in progress, Rome had just suffered a terrible defeat off the north-western point of Sicily, at Drepana, a defeat all the more hideous because it was supposed to have been caused by the impiety of the Consul Clodius, who, hearing that the sacred chickens would not eat, perpetrated his grim jest by saying "let them drink then instead," and drowning them all. But to cap it all the wall of Rome was [Pg 89] struck by lightning. Then action was necessary and the books were consulted. They ordered that sacrifice should be made to Dis and Proserpina, a black steer to Dis, and a black cow to Proserpina, three successive nights, out on the Campus Martius, at an altar which was called the *Tarentum,* and that the ceremony should be repeated at the end of a hundred years. Here the myth-makers of later times have been even more busily at work than they were in the case of Aesculapius. The Aesculapius story was fitted out by them merely with a few miraculous details, a few legendary ornaments, but the story of Dis and Proserpina was so covered with their fabrications that it has only recently been freed from them and seen in its true light, and certain phases were so absolutely perverted that there are still a number of very difficult points. To get a clear understanding of the situation we must begin quite a distance back.

Taken as a whole, religious beliefs are among the most conservative things in the world; the individual may grow as radical as you please, but his effect on the general religious consciousness of his time is extremely slight. Occasionally the number of radical individuals grows larger and certain classes of society are affected by their views, but even, in the periods of religious development which we are apt to think of as most iconoclastic, society taken in the large, and on the average of all classes, is not much more [Pg 90] radical than in apparently normal times. And while religion as a whole is conservative, there is one section of it more conservative than all the rest, a section from which change is almost excluded, that is the beliefs concerning the dead. In our discussion of the religion of Numa we saw the very primitive character of Roman beliefs in this field, the firm retention of the old animistic idea of the dead, the tendency to class the dead together as a mass and to believe in a collective rather than an individual immortality, and above all the abhorrence of the dead and the disinclination to dwell on their condition and to paint imaginary pictures of life beyond the grave. In view of these feelings it is not strange that we have great difficulty in finding any old Roman gods of the dead, aside from the dead who are themselves all gods. These dead as gods (*Di Manes*) and possibly Mother Earth (*Terra Mater*) are the only rulers in the Lower World. In Greece on the contrary death was almost as natural as life, and though the conditions in early times were not unlike those in Rome, as Rohde in his *Psyche* has so wonderfully described them, the Greek soon grew beyond this, and the world of the dead became almost as well known to him as the world of the living. There was a kingdom of the dead, and a king and queen ruled over them. These rulers were called by different names in different parts of Greece, but the names which they had in certain parts of [Pg 91] the Peloponnesus, Hades the king of the dead and Persephone his bride, were destined to survive the rest. The cult of this royal pair travelled far and wide, but its most notable development occurred in Attica, where Persephone became Kore the daughter of Demeter, stolen by Hades to become his bride, while Hades himself under the sunny skies of Athens lost some of his terrors and became Pluto, the god of riches, especially the rich blessings of the earth. But all this was very foreign to Rome, and while the Greeks were thinking these thoughts, the Romans were going quietly along, content with their simple *Di Manes*. No better proof of this can be desired than the one accidentally given us in the introduction of Demeter and her daughter Kore into Rome as Ceres and Libera in B.C. 493, and the absolute colourlessness and pointlessness of Libera, in a word the entire lack of connexion in the religious consciousness of Rome between Libera and Persephone. But in B.C. 249, almost two and a half centuries later, matters were on a different basis; Rome had been learning a great deal that was foreign to her old beliefs, and there was no longer anything impossible to her in the idea of individual rulers of the dead. Thus at the command of the books Pluto and Persephone were received into the state-cult, though the strangeness of the situation was acknowledged, at least in so far that they translated Pluto into the Latin Dis; Persephone to be sure was left [Pg 92] alone, or more strictly speaking was accommodated to the Latin tongue by being changed to Proserpina. It is of course impossible that the Romans of B.C. 249 were entirely ignorant of Pluto and Persephone until the Sibylline books bade them be brought in. Here again the traders from Southern Italy had been their teachers; and the name *Tarentum* of the altar where the sacrifice was to be made may possibly indicate the town of Tarentum as the source of the cult. The Romans knew Tarentum only too well since the eventful war with Pyrrhus, which lay only a generation back in their history.

And so the Romans adopted the Greek gods of the dead, and thus, at least theoretically, put their dead ancestors into subjection to the Greeks just as they themselves, the descendants, were sitting at the feet of the Greeks in this life. But though the enactment of the Senate gave these gods Roman citizenship, and the priests of the Sibylline books were in duty bound to perform the ritual of the cult, be it said to the credit of the Romans, the gods themselves never took a very deep hold of the religious life of the people in general. Their names, to be sure, crept into a few of the old formulae and stood side by side with the older deities, and Proserpina was made much of by the Roman poets; but the real tests of devotion, dedicatory inscriptions, are almost entirely absent. Strangely enough the only thing which seems to [Pg 93] have caught their fancy was the weird ritual of the nightly sacrifice at the Tarentum, and especially its repetition after one hundred years. This idea of the hundred years is Roman rather than Greek, and it is at least open to question whether it may not have been added to the instructions in the oracle to give the whole matter an added Roman colour. Thus in B.C. 249 were instituted the Secular Games, which were repeated with approximate accuracy in B.C. 146, and would doubtless have been again between B.C. 49 and 46, had not the Civil War completely filled men's minds and made human sacrifices to the dead, in battle, an almost daily occurrence. Meantime the Roman annalists were working backwards in their own peculiar fashion, and building out into the past a series of fictitious celebrations preceding B.C. 249, one hundred years apart, back into the time of the kingdom. On the other hand we shall have occasion later to speak of the restoration of the games and their reorganisation by Augustus.

Under the test of adversity nations are very much like individuals, and a national weakness, which is often entirely concealed in normal conditions, comes prominently and disastrously to the surface in the hour when strength is most needed. The war with Hannibal was just such a crisis in Rome's history, and under its influence Rome's dependence upon the Sibylline books was more [Pg 94] pronounced than ever. The seeds of superstition sown during the earlier centuries burst now into full blossom, destined to produce the fruit, the gathering of which was to be the bitter task of the closing centuries of the republic. The story of the Second Punic War, regarded merely from the military standpoint, reads for Rome almost like a nightmare, with its long succession of apparently easy victories turning one by one into defeats; but when we add to this that other chronicle, of which Livy is equally fond, the long lists of portents and prodigies sent by the angered gods, and when we realise that to the masses of the people the wrath of the gods was more terrible and just as real as the hostility of Hannibal, then we have not the heart to reproach them for their religious frenzy. Seen by themselves, the jumping of a cow out of a second-story window, or the images of the gods shedding tears, do not seem very serious matters, but endow us with three hundred years of hereditary dread of these things, give us the instinctive interpretation of them as the turning away from us of the powers upon which we rely for help, nay their positive opposition to us and our hopes—and our condition in the presence of these phenomena would be very different.

Thus almost every year between B.C. 218 and 201 had its share of religious ceremonial, and the Sibylline books, which had hitherto been, in theory [Pg 95] at least, merely an alternative method of religious procedure permitted to exist alongside of the older and more conservative forms, became now the order of the day. Like a Homeric picture in which the quarrels of the gods in Olympus run parallel to the battles of Greeks and Trojans on the plains of Troy, so every victory which Rome won over Hannibal on the field of battle was bought at the price of a victory of Greek gods over Roman gods in the field of religion; and further, although Rome succeeded in keeping Hannibal outside of her own walls, her gods did not succeed in defending the *pomerium* against the Greek gods, and it is during this Second Punic War that this, the greatest safeguard of old Roman religion and customs, was broken down, and the new gods gained entire possession of the city, placing their temples on the spots hitherto held most sacred. From now on all distinction ceases, and it is scarcely possible to speak of a Roman in contrast to a Graeco-Roman cult. It is important however to observe that this break-down occurred because of excess of religious zeal rather than through neglect and indifference, and though we may indeed notice a gradual deterioration of the deities introduced by the books, all the way down from the busy working gods like Ceres and Mercury and Neptune to the more miraculous Aesculapius, and the cult of Dis or Proserpina with its possibilities of weird fantastic [Pg 96] worship, there have been however as yet only scanty traces of the orgiastic element. But this was the next step, and it was not long in coming. The rapid campaigns of the earlier years of the war with Hannibal had passed, Cannae (B.C. 216) had been somewhat retrieved by Metaurus (B.C. 207), where the reinforcements for Hannibal, led by Hasdrubal, had been cut to pieces, but the result was not what had been hoped for, and Hannibal had not left Italy, but entrenched in the mountains of the south he seemed to be preparing to pass the rest of his life there. It was in this the year B.C. 205 that the help of the books was again sought, if peradventure they might show the way to drive Hannibal out of the country. The reply came that, when a foreign-born enemy should wage war upon the land, he could be conquered and driven from Italy, if the Great Mother of the gods should be brought to Rome from Phrygia. The rest of the story is so quaintly and withal so truthfully told by Livy (Bk. xxix.) that it will not be amiss to quote his words:—"The oracle discovered by the Decemviri affected the Senate the more on this account because the ambassadors who had brought the gifts [vowed at the battle of Metaurus] to Delphi reported that when they were sacrificing to the Pythian Apollo the omens were all favourable, and that the oracle had given response that a greater victory was at hand for the Roman people [Pg 97] than that one from whose spoils they were then bringing gifts. And as a finishing touch to this same hope they dwelt upon the prophetic opinion of Publius Scipio regarding the end of the war, because he had asked for Africa as his province. And so in order that they might the more quickly obtain that victory which promised itself to them by the omens and oracles of fate, they began to consider what means there was of bringing the goddess to Rome. As yet the Roman people had no states in alliance with them in Asia Minor; however they remembered that formerly Aesculapius had been brought from Greece for the sake of the health of the people, though they had no alliance with Greece. They realised too that a friendship had been begun with King Attalus [of Pergamon] ... and that Attalus would do what he could in behalf of the Roman people; and so they decided to send ambassadors to him, ... and they allotted them five ships-of-war in order that they might approach in a fitting manner the countries which they desired to interest in their favour. Now when the ambassadors were on their way to Asia they disembarked at Delphi, and approaching the oracle asked what prospect it offered them and the Roman people of accomplishing the things which they had been sent to do. It is said that the reply was that through King Attalus they would obtain what they sought, but that when [Pg 98] they brought the goddess to Rome they should see to it that the best man in Rome should be at hand to receive her. Then they came to Pergamon to the king [Attalus], and he received them graciously and led them to Pessinus in Phrygia, and he gave over to them the sacred stone which, the natives said, was the Mother of the gods, and bade them carry it to Rome. And Marcus Valerius Falto was sent ahead by the ambassadors and he announced that the goddess was coming, and that the best man in the state must be sought out to receive her with due ceremony." In the next year (B.C. 204) after recounting new prodigies Livy continues:—"Then too the matter of the Idaean Mother must be attended to, for aside from the fact that Marcus Valerius, one of the ambassadors who had been sent ahead, had announced that she would soon be in Italy, there was also a fresh message that she was already at Tarracina. The Senate had to decide a very important matter, namely who was the best man in the state, for every man in the state preferred a victory in such a contest as this to any commands or offices which the vote of the Senate or the people might give him. They decided that of all the good men in the state the best was Publius Scipio.... He then with all the matrons was ordered to go to Ostia to meet the goddess and to receive her from the ship, to carry her to land and to give her over to [Pg 99] the women to carry. After the ship came to the mouth of the Tiber, Scipio, going out in a small boat, as he had been commanded, received the goddess from the priests and carried her to land. And the noblest women of the land ... received her ... and they carried the goddess in their arms, taking turn about while all Rome poured out to meet her, and incense-burners were placed before the doors where she was carried by, and incense was burned in her honour. And thus praying that she might enter willingly and propitiously into the city, they carried her into the temple of Victory, which is on the Palatine, on the day before the Nones of April [April 4]. And this was a festal day and the people in great numbers gave gifts to the goddess, and a banquet for the gods was held, and games were performed which were called *Megalesia*." This extraordinary picture is probably in the main historically correct. The most striking part of it, the enthusiasm of the Roman populace, is certainly not overdrawn. Thus was introduced into Rome the last deity ever summoned by means of the books, the one whose cult was destined to outlast that of all the others, and to do more harm and produce more demoralisation than all the other cults together. To understand why this was so, we must go back for a moment.

The influence of Greece on Rome was progressive, and we are able to indicate at least three distinct [Pg 100] periods and phases of it, so far as religion is concerned: first, the informal coming of a few Greek gods who adapted themselves more or less completely to the old Roman character; such are Hercules and Castor and even Apollo, though Apollo was indirectly responsible for the second period, because he was the cause of the coming of the Sibylline books. The influence of these books produced the second period, with its characteristics of ever-growing superstition, and greater pomp in cult acts, but though the sobriety of the old days had changed into a restless activity, the new gods who came in and the new cult acts introduced were still of such a character that Romans could take part in the worship without shame. But just as the staid Apollo had produced the books, so now as their last bequest the books brought in the Great Mother, and the third period had begun, the period of orgiastic Oriental worship, which prevailed, at least among certain classes, until the establishment of Christianity. We may well ask who this Great Mother was, and why this one Greek cult should be so different from all the rest.

At different points in Asia Minor and in Crete a goddess was worshipped, originally without proper name, as the great source of all fertility, the mother of all things, even of the gods. Mount Dindymos in Phrygia was one of the chief centres of the cult, and there the Great Mother was known also as [Pg 101] Cybele. From these various centres the cult spread over all the Greek world, but wherever it went, it always gave evidence of its birthplace by certain strange Oriental elements both in its myths and in its rites. Its devotees were a noisy orgiastic band, who filled the streets with their dances, and the air with their singing and the clashing of their symbols, to the accompaniment of the rattling of coin in the money box—for the collection of money from the bystanders was always a part of the performance.

This then was what the "best man in the state" and the grave Roman matrons went forth from Rome to receive—a sacred stone representing the goddess, and a band of noisy emasculated priests; and this was what they opened their gates to, and took up into their holy of holies, the Palatine hill, the birthplace of Rome. The Greeks had again come bearing gifts, and like the Trojans who broke down their walls and took the wooden horse up into their citadel, Romans, the reputed descendents of these Trojans, were carrying up to their most sacred hill another gift of Greece which was to capture their city. They put the image in the temple of Victoria on the Palatine until such time as its own temple was ready to receive it, and the goddess of Victory seemed to respond to its presence, for did not Hannibal leave Italy the very next year? And who would be so impious as to suggest that to Scipio and not Cybele belonged the glory, and that [Pg 102] a strong Roman army in Africa affected Hannibal more than a sacred stone on the Palatine?

It may well be doubted whether anything but such a great exigency would ever have induced Rome to accept such an utterly foreign cult; and when the nightmare of the war was past, the Senate awoke to the realisation that a very serious act had been committed. To their credit be it said that they did what they could to minimise the evil. The goddess had brought her own priests with her, the cult was in their hands, and there the law decreed it must stay, and no Roman citizen could become a priest. That this law was really enforced is shown by several cases where punishment, even transportation across the sea, was meted out to transgressors. Then too the worship must be in the main confined to the precincts of the temple on the Palatine, and only on certain days of the year were the priests allowed to perform in the streets of the city. It is significant of the strength of Roman law that these enactments held good for three and a half centuries, and were not changed until the reign of Antoninus Pius.

In the introduction of the Great Mother the Sibylline books performed their last and most notable achievement. Hereafter they introduced no new deities, and were consulted only occasionally, chiefly for political purposes, for example in B.C. 87 against the followers of Sulla, and in B.C. 56 in connexion [Pg 103] with a scheme of purely political import. Their work was done, and we have seen in what it consisted. For three hundred years they had been encouraging the growth of superstition. From their vantage ground of the temple of Juppiter Optimus Maximus, the essence of all that was most patriotically Roman in Rome, they had been giving forth these infallible oracles which seemed so much superior to the simple "yes and no" answers with which the old Romans had been content in their dealings with the gods. In times of peril by pestilence and by battle they had given advice, and the pestilence had ceased and the battle had turned to victory. It seemed indeed that the Sibyl deserved the gratitude of Rome. Time alone could teach them what the books had really given them. It was only in the coming generations that it became evident that the abuse of faith, the substitution of incantation for devotion, was destructive of true religion. It is the effect of this substitution on the various classes of society under the new and trying social conditions of the last two centuries of the republic that forms the theme of our next chapter.

[Pg 104]

THE DECLINE OF FAITH

It is the fashion of our day to think no evil of Greece. In art we are experiencing another Renaissance, not like that of the fourteenth and fifteenth centuries in a revival of ancient Rome, but in a movement leading behind Rome to the classic and even the pre-classic models of Greece. In itself it is a healthful tendency, a needed corrective to the sensational search for novelty which characterised the closing years of the nineteenth century. But in our admiration for the Greek spirit we ought not to forget that after Alexander that spirit lost much of its beauty, and aged very rapidly. We may indeed regret the fact that Rome, like certain persons of our acquaintance, seemed at times to possess a strong faculty for assimilating the worst of her surroundings, while occasionally curiously unresponsive to the better things; and yet we ought in justice to strive to realise the fact that not only is the Greek spirit at its best an unteachable thing, but that at the historical moment when Rome came under that influence the Greek world was very old and weary. [Pg 105] It was Rome's misfortune and not her fault that when she was old enough to go to school, Alexandrianism with its pedantic detail was the order of the day in mythology, and the timorous post-Socratic schools were the teachers of philosophy. Naturally if Rome had been another Greece she would have worked back from these later forms to the truer, purer spirit, but Rome was not Greece, and no thoughtful man ever pretended that she was. In the third century before Christ Greece began actively to influence Rome; before that time Hellenic influence had been confined largely to the effects on religion produced by the Sibylline books, and to the effects on society caused by the presence of Greek traders. But now Greek thought as embodied in the literature began to affect Roman thought, and to bring into being a literature based on Greek models. Three centuries of Sibylline oracles had produced for Rome the pathological religious condition of the Second Punic War, when she did not think twice before breaking down the religious barrier which had hitherto separated the national from the adopted elements in her religion, and at the same time unhesitatingly reached out to Asia Minor for an Oriental cult, masquerading in Greek colours, and placed on the Palatine the Great Mother of Pessinus. From this time on two influences were steadily at work which shaped the history of Roman religion in the two remaining centuries till the close [Pg 106] of the republic: one, mythology, directly affecting the forms of the cult and the beliefs concerning the individual gods; the other, philosophy, attacking the whole foundation of religious belief in general.

Greece gave her gods to Rome when she herself was weary of them, she gave her the tired gods, exhausted by centuries of handling, long ago dragged down from Olympus, and weary with serving as lay-figures for poets and artists, and being for ever rigged out in new mythological garments, or jaded with the laboratory experiments of philosophers who tried to interpret them in every conceivable fashion or else to do away with them entirely. It is no wonder that it did not take the Romans more than a century to come to the end of these gods, to find that the only one among them who could satisfy their religious desires was the least Greek of them all, the Magna Mater, and having found this to go forth to take to themselves more like unto her, in a word, to crave the sensational cults of the Orient. And the philosophy which Greece gave Rome was no better than the mythology. It is not strange that human thought experienced a reaction after a century which contained both Plato and Aristotle, but it is a pity that Rome should have learned her philosophy from a period of doubt and scepticism, an age in which the lesser masters, who had known the greater ones, had gone, leaving nothing but pupils' pupils. [Pg 107]

The history of religion in Rome during the last two centuries of the republic is the story of the action and reaction of these two tendencies—the one toward the novel and sensational in worship, which we may call superstition, the other the philosophy of doubt, which we may call scepticism—in the presence of the established religion of the state. This much the two centuries have in common, but here their resemblance ends. In the first of these centuries (B.C. 200-100) the state religion was able to hold her own, at least in outward appearance, and to wage war against both tendencies. In the other century (B.C. 100 to Augustus) politics gained control of the state religion and so robbed her of her strength that she was crushed between the opposing forces of superstition and scepticism. It is to the story of the earlier of these two centuries, the second before Christ, that we now turn.

With the close of the Second Punic War there began for Rome a period of very great material prosperity. This prosperity was, to be sure, not exactly distributed, and it is not without its resemblance to some of our modern instances of commercial prosperity, in that it was not so much a general bettering of economic conditions as the very rapid increase of the wealth of a relatively small number, an increase gained at the expense of positive detriment to a large element in the popula [Pg 108] tion. Thus it was that a century of which the first seventy years provide an almost unparalleled spectacle of the increase of national territory, accompanied, according to the ancient methods of taxation, by a vast increase in national wealth, should close with the tragedies of Tiberius and Gaius Gracchus and the legacy of class hatred which produced the civil wars. This growth in wealth and territory was not without its effects on the outward appearance of the state religion. The territory was gained by a series of minor wars in the course of which many temples were vowed; and the spoils of the war provided the means for the fulfilment of the vows. Thus to the outward observer it might well have seemed that the religion of the state was enjoying a time of great prosperity. Between the close of the Punic War (B.C. 201) and the year of Tiberius Gracchus (B.C. 133) we have accurate knowledge of the dedication of no less than nineteen state temples, and there were undoubtedly many others of which we have no record. Another apparently good sign is the fact that the Sibylline books are silent, so far as the introduction of new deities is concerned. Yet these surface indications are deceptive. As for the Sibylline books, now that the *pomerium* line had been broken down, and the temples of Greek gods might be placed anywhere in the city, it was a very simple matter for the state to bring in any Greek god that it pleased, and likening him to a [Pg 109] more or less similar Roman god and calling him by the Roman name, to put up a temple to him anywhere. It was also true that, as Roman theology was now based on the principle that every Roman god had his Greek parallel and *vice versa*, there were no gods left, whose names would have occurred at all in the Sibylline books, who could not be brought in now without them. And as for the vowing of new temples, this represented at best merely the habit formed during more devout days; religion was moving by the momentum acquired during the Second Punic War, and the gods to whom these temples were erected were really Greek gods under Roman names. In a word, not only was the state religion becoming more and more of a form day by day, but the form was that of Greece and not of Rome. It is extremely interesting to trace this movement in detail, to look behind the outward appearance and see the remarkable changes that were really taking place.

If we look at the temples which were built in the years following the Second Punic War, we shall have no difficulty in finding examples of the introduction of Greek gods under Roman names. During the war itself in the year B.C. 207 a Roman general had vowed a temple to Juventas on the occasion of a battle near Siena. Juventas was an old Roman goddess, one of those abstract deities which had been produced by the breaking off and becoming [Pg 110] independent of a cult-title. She was intimately associated with Juppiter, and had a special shrine in the Capitoline temple. Juventas was the divine representative of the putting away of childish things and the assumption of the responsibilities and privileges of young manhood. This act was symbolised by the Romans in the beautiful ceremony of putting on the toga of manhood (*toga virilis*), when the lad was led by his father to the Capitoline temple to make sacrifices to Juppiter, and at the same time a contribution was made to the treasury of Juventas. But this was not the goddess in whose honour the temple vowed at Siena was built at the Circus Maximus and dedicated B.C. 191. This Juventas was nothing more or less than the Greek Hebe, the female counterpart of Ganymedes, as cupbearer to the gods. Similarly in B.C. 179 a temple was dedicated to Diana at the Circus Flaminius, but this was not the old goddess of Aricia, whose cult Rome had adopted for the sake of increasing her influence in the Latin league. It was the Greek Artemis, who at her first coming into Rome had been associated with Apollo in the temple built in B.C. 431, and was now given a temple of her own. Perhaps the strangest of all is the temple which was erected to Mars in the Campus Martius in B.C. 138. It might well be supposed that the Romans would keep holy the reputed father of their race, the god to whom, under Juppiter, their [Pg 111] success was due. On the contrary in B.C. 217, when they were carrying out a Greek ceremony of offering a banquet to a set of gods, arranged in pairs, they showed no hesitation in grouping together Mars and Venus to represent the

Greek pair Ares and Aphrodite, thus doing violence to Mars by bringing him into a relationship with Venus which was entirely foreign to old Roman thought, and identifying him with Ares, with whom he had nothing to do. Now in B.C. 138 a temple is built to Ares under the name of Mars, close beside the venerable old altar of Mars, one of the oldest and most sacred of Roman shrines.

But this passion for identifying Greek gods with Roman ones did not confine itself to finding a parallel for the greater gods of Greece; and less known deities were introduced into Rome in the same way. The old Roman god, Faunus, in whose honour the ancient festival of the *Lupercalia* was yearly celebrated, had as his associate a goddess, Fauna, who was better known as the "good goddess" (Bona Dea). Eventually this new title Bona Dea crowded out the old title Fauna, so that it was almost entirely forgotten. Bona Dea was a goddess of women, and the most characteristic feature of her worship was the exclusion of men from taking part in it. Now there was a Greek goddess, called Damia, also a goddess of women, from whose cult also men were excluded, and her cult spread from [Pg 112] Greece to the Greek colonies of Southern Italy, especially Tarentum, and so eventually to Rome. But by the time she arrived in Rome the connexion of Fauna and Bona Dea had been entirely forgotten. Damia was surely a Bona Dea, yes she was *the* Bona Dea, for was not the proof at hand in the fact that men were excluded from both cults? So a temple was built for her, probably shortly after the Second Punic War, and from the time no one ever thought of poor Fauna again, except scholars and poets, who amused themselves, as was their wont, by putting her in various genealogical relationships to Faunus, as sister, wife, or daughter, while Damia lived and prospered under the stolen title of the Bona Dea.

We see from this on what a small resemblance such identifications were based, in this case merely on the presence of a similar minor injunction in the laws of each cult. But we have here at least a genuine cult which had arrived and was asking for admission, and in so far we are better off than in most instances, where nothing substantial was gained by the identification. Two forces were now at work assisting in this fusion of Greek and Roman gods, namely art and literature. The capture of Syracuse marked an epoch in Rome's artistic career; for several centuries she had employed Greek architects and had also become acquainted with the artistic types of certain Greek gods, but now all at once a [Pg 113] wealth of Greek sculpture was disclosed to her, and she could not rest content until all her gods were represented in the fashion of man. The adoption of the Greek type, in those cases where an identification had already been effected, was not difficult and was in the main successful, though there followed almost inevitably an enrichment of the Greek element in the Roman god because of the presence of some attribute in the statue, which brought its own myth with it. But there were certain Roman gods for whom Greek parallels could not be found, and in these cases a compromise, usually rather an awkward one, had to be effected, as for example when the Roman gods of the storeroom, the *Di Penates*, were represented by statues of the Greek Castor and Pollux. In such cases confusion was sure to follow, and subsequent antiquarians would be tempted to write treatises proving the original connexion of Castor or Pollux with the Penates, as gods of protection in general, etc. Literature too in its own way was fully as misleading, and Roman scholars became fascinated with the labyrinths of Alexandrian mythology, and straightway began to build Roman myths as rapidly as possible, establishing lists of old Latin kings and all sorts of genealogies, and weaving as many Greek mythological figures as possible into the legends of the foundation of Italic towns.

It was the ceremonial of the cult however which most often offered the best means of identification, [Pg 114] as we have seen above in the case of Bona Dea-Damia, where the exclusion of men from the rites was the main point of similarity. In a similar way the old Roman god of the harvest, Consus, was identified with the Greek ocean-god Poseidon because horse-races were a characteristic feature of the festivals of each; and the old Roman goddess of women and of childbirth was given as her Greek parallel the Greek goddess Leukothea, the helper of those in peril at sea, because in both cases slaves were forbidden to take part in the cult.

But the effect of the capture of Rome by these Greek gods and Greek ceremonials was not confined to the mere addition of new ideas, and the transformation of certain old Roman deities. This would have been comparatively harmless, but there was inevitably another result: the consequent neglect of all Roman deities for whom no Greek parallels were forthcoming, and the forgetting of all the original Roman ideas which were crowded into the background by the novel and more brilliant Greek ideas. Even the festivals of the old Roman year were treated in the same cavalier manner. The interest of the people continued only with those ceremonies which frightened them or pleased them. There were certain festivals, for example the *Lupercalia,* the old ceremony of purification on February 15, for which a reverence was still felt; and others like the *Parilia,* the birthday of Rome, on April 21, [Pg 115] or the Anna Perenna festival on March 15, which involved open-air celebrations and picnics. These and others like them were always kept up, while many others were totally neglected. Naturally for the present the forms were continued by the state; the festivals were celebrated at least by the priests; and every temple received sacrifice on its birthday. The wheels of the state religion were still running, but the power behind them had stopped, and it was only momentum which kept them in motion.

It is only when we realise these things that we can understand how it was possible that the most learned scholars at the close of the republic were so desperately ignorant concerning old Roman religion. In regard to many of the old Roman gods they know absolutely nothing, and try to disguise their ignorance behind a show of learning based on etymological sleight-of-hand; in regard to the rest their information is so tangled with Greek ideas that it is often almost impossible to unravel the mass and separate the old from the new. This unravelling has been the tedious occupation of the last half century in the study of Roman religion; and so patiently and successfully has it been accomplished that, although we would give almost anything for a few books of Varro's *Divine Antiquities*, it is tolerably certain that the possession of these books would not change in the least the fundamental concepts underlying the modern re [Pg 116] construction of ancient Roman religion; though it is equally certain that these books would emphasise just so much more strongly, what we already realise, that this modern reconstruction is in distinct contradiction to many of Varro's favourite theories. It is an accomplishment of which History may well be modestly proud, that modern scholars have been able to eliminate, to a large degree, the personal equation and the myopic effects of his own time from the statements of the greatest scholar of Roman antiquity, and thus though handicapped by the possession of merely a small percentage of the facts which Varro knew, to arrive at a concept of the whole matter infinitely more correct than that which his books contained.

During this second century before Christ, therefore, the state religion was apparently unchanged so far as the outward form was concerned. The terminology and the ceremonies were much the same as before, but the content was quite different: Greek gods and Greek ideas had displaced Roman gods and Roman ideas, and the official representatives of religion, the state priests, were carrying the whole burden of worship on their own shoulders, because popular interest had been in the main deflected and was working along other lines. These lines of rival interest were superstition and scepticism, phenomena which at first sight appear as distinct opposites, but which are on the contrary very closely akin, so that [Pg 117] they usually occur together not only in the same age, but frequently even in the same individual. They are purely relative terms, and the essence of superstition consists in its surplus element, just as the essence of scepticism lies in its deficiency. No religion judged from the standpoint of the worshipper can properly be called a superstition, but if once we can establish the essential things in a religion, then any large addition to those essential things savours of superstition. Speaking with historical sympathy we have no right therefore to designate early Roman religion as a superstition—it may of course be relatively so in comparison with other religious forms—but once we have established the essential elements in that early religion, we may consider the introduction of new and entirely different elements as superstition. The old religion of Rome consisted in the exact and scrupulous fulfilment of a large number of minute ceremonials. The result of this careful fulfilment of ritual was that the powers around man did him no harm but rather good, and that was the end of the whole matter. Religion did not command or even permit special inquiries into these powers; it was not only not man's duty to try to know the gods, it was his positive duty to try not to. Through the influence of Greece there had now come into Rome an altogether new idea, nourished largely by the Sibylline books, and represented most fully in the Magna Mater, the idea [Pg 118] of the perpetual service of a god, a consecration to him, to the exclusion of all other things, and a life given over to the orgiastic performance of cult acts, which produced a state of ecstasy and consequently a communion with the deity. Along with this there went a belief in the possibility, by means of certain books and certain men, of obtaining from the gods a knowledge of the future. It is these surplus beliefs, quite contrary to the spirit of old Roman religion, which may justly be called superstition.

The Sibylline books had aroused these feelings, a knowledge of the oracle at Delphi had increased them, the rites of Aesculapius had carried them farther, but it was not until the Magna Mater came that they seem to have burst forth in any large degree. But aside from the rapid growth of the Magna Mater cult itself we have in this second century two instances of this tendency. The first was connected with the god Dionysos-Liber, innocent enough at his first reception in B.C. 493, in the company of Demeter-Ceres and Kore-Libera. To be sure the state had introduced him merely as the god of wine, but the mystery element in Dionysos took firm hold on private worship, and the Bacchanalian clubs or societies began to spread over Italy. In the course of about three centuries they had become a formidable menace to the morals and even the physical security of the inhabitants of Rome. Their meetings instead of occurring three times a year [Pg 119] took place five times a month, and finally in B.C. 186 the famous Bacchanalian trial took place, of which Livy (Bk. xxxix.) gives such a graphic account, and to which a copy of the inscription of the decree of the Senate, preserved to our day, gives such eloquent testimony, providing as it does severe penalties for subsequent offenders, and recognising on the other hand large liberty of conscience.

The same love of mystery and longing for knowledge which produced the Bacchanalian clubs accorded a warm reception to astrology and made men listen with eagerness to those who could tell their fortunes or guide their lives by means of the stars. We do not know when the bearers of this knowledge first arrived in Rome, but Cato, in his *Farm Almanac*, our earliest piece of prose literature, in giving rules for the behaviour of the farm bailiff especially enjoins the intending landowner that his bailiff should not be given to the consultation of Chaldaean astrologers. Within half a century the problem of the Chaldaeans grew so serious that state interference was necessary, and in B.C. 139 the praetor Cn. Cornelius Hispalus issued an edict ordering the Chaldaeans to leave Rome and Italy within ten days.

The same age which produced this growth of superstition brought also the antidote for it in the shape of a sceptical philosophy, but the only trouble was that this philosophy not only cured [Pg 120] superstition but in doing so killed the genuine religious spirit underlying it. It cast out, to be sure, the seven devils of superstition, but when men returned to themselves again, they found their whole spiritual house swept and garnished. With the death of the direct pupils of Aristotle, the Greek mind had thought out all the problems of philosophy of which man at that time was able to conceive. The following generations of philosophers devoted themselves either to the elaboration of detail or to a renewed examination of the foundations of belief, with the result that their smaller minds came to smaller conclusions, and the end of their investigations was one increased scepticism. The schools of the day showed many slight variations and bore many different names, but they all agreed in being more or less pervaded by a sceptical spirit, and by accenting ethics as against metaphysics, though they defined ethics very differently according to their starting point.

One of the earliest philosophical influences which reached Rome was however that of a pre-Socratic school, the school of Pythagoras. This was natural enough in itself, as the headquarters of the school was in Southern Italy, but it is curious and significant that the first pronounced instance of its influence occurred shortly after the Second Punic War, and in connexion with a clever fraud which was perpetrated with a view to influencing religion. In the year [Pg 121] B.C. 181 a certain man reported that when he was ploughing his field, which lay on the other side of the Tiber, at the foot of the Janiculum, the plough had laid bare two stone sarcophagi, stoutly sealed with lead, and bearing inscriptions in Greek and Latin according to which they purported to contain, one of them the body of King Numa, the other, his writings. When they were opened the one which ought to have contained the body was empty, in the other lay two rolls, each roll consisting of seven books; the one set of seven was written in Latin and treated of pontifical law, the other consisted of philosophical writings. They were examined, found to be heretical and subversive to true religion, and were accordingly burned in the Comitium. The connexion of Numa and Pythagoras, historically impossible but believed in at this time, makes it practically certain that this was a clever attempt to introduce the philosophy of Pythagoras into Rome under the holy sanction of the name of Numa. Fortunately the zeal of the city praetor frustrated the scheme. But the doctrines of philosophy, which thus failed to enter by the door of religion, found the door of literature wide open for them. As the irony of fate would have it, Cato, the stalwart enemy of Greek influence, had brought back from Sardinia with him the poet Ennius, and at about the time when the false books of Numa were burning in the Comitium Ennius was giving to the world a Latin [Pg 122] translation of the *Sacred History* of the Greek Euhemerus. This Euhemerus, a Sicilian who had lived about a century before this time, earned his title to fame by writing a novel of adventure and travel, in which he described a trip which he had taken in the Red Sea along the coast of Arabia to the wonderful island of Panchaia, where he found a column with an inscription on it telling the life history of Ouranos, Kronos, and Zeus, who were thus shown to have been historical characters afterwards elevated into deities. It was this theological element in his book which made him famous. This theory of the historical origin of the gods is even today called Euhemerism, and has exerted a baleful influence over writers on mythology from its author's day down to our own. These then were the doctrines which Ennius presented to the Romans in their own tongue, and it is pathetic to realise that his *Sacred History* formed the first formal treatise on theology which Rome ever possessed. Born under such an evil star, it is small wonder that her theological speculations never reached great metaphysical heights.

In these days it seemed to the Senate that the question of philosophy was beginning to be so serious that it might be considered as a public danger, and that it was therefore their duty to try to cope with it. They chose, of course, the typical Roman method of dealing with such matters, and [Pg 123] the philosophers were expelled from Rome. At first in B.C. 173 it was only the Epicureans who were sent out, but in B.C. 161 the edict was broadened to include philosophers in general. However six years later, in B.C. 155, there came to Rome an embassy of philosophers whose mission was avowedly political and not philosophical, and who thus could not be excluded, while at the same time they took occasion to preach their philosophical doctrines. It was fortunate for Rome that Stoicism, the best among all these philosophies, appealed to her most strongly and became thus the national philosophy of Rome. Stoicism was in many respects quite as sceptical as the others, but it had at least this great advantage that it laid a strong emphasis on ethics, and was in so far capable of becoming a guide of life. It might be well enough for Greeks, whose aggressive work in the world had been done, to settle down to an idle old age with a theory of life which practically excluded the possibility of strong decisive action, but Rome was still young, and most of her work was still before her. She might think herself very old and pretend to take peculiar delight in many of the more decadent forms of Greek thought, but in reality her leaders instinctively turned to Stoicism, as affording a compromise between the mere thoughtless activity of youth, which acts for the love of acting, and the jaded philosophy of the vanity of [Pg 124] all effort. About the middle of the century (*circa* B.C. 150) there existed in Rome a centre of culture and intellectual influence, a little group of men peculiarly interesting, because they form practically the first instance of an intellectual coterie in the history of Rome. Their leader was the younger Scipio, who had as his associates his friend Laelius, the poet Lucilius, whose brilliant writings, submerged by the more brilliant satires of Horace, form one of the most deplorable losses in Roman literature, and the Stoic philosopher Panaitios of Rhodes. Terence had also belonged to the circle, but he was now dead. Stoicism was the avowed philosophy of these men, and their influence, especially that of Panaitios and Lucilius, did much to popularise their chosen philosophical creed.

While Stoicism claimed superiority to religion and showed the impossibility of attaching any value to religious knowledge, it recognised the necessity of religion for the common people on grounds of expediency, and effected a reconciliation between this denial of religion on the one hand, and the recognition of it on the other, by asserting that the religion of the state was justified not only by expediency but much more by the fact that it was after all only the presentation of the truths of Stoicism in a form which was intelligible to the lower classes. Had this group of Scipio and his associates made an effort to emphasise these [Pg 125] particular doctrines of Stoicism in relation to religion, the downfall of the state religion, which occurred in the following century, might have been hindered. But for reasons, which we shall see in a moment, this downfall could not have been prevented, and it is doubtful whether the influence of any philosophical system, even when supported by such prominent men, could have perceptibly postponed the catastrophe. Meantime the only visible contribution of Stoicism to the problem of religion was the growth under her influence of the idea of a "double truth," one truth for the intellectual classes and one for the common people, reaching its climax in the phrase "It is expedient for the state to be deceived in matters of religion" (*expedit igitur falli in religione civitatem*). This was the attitude toward religion of the most intellectual men in the community at the beginning of what was in many ways the most terrible period in Rome's history.

The last century before Christ (more exactly B.C. 133-B.C. 27) is the story of how Rome became an empire because she was no longer able to be a republic; it is the history of the growth of one-man power because many-men power had become impossible. This growth was caused not only, nor at first even chiefly, by the grasping character of Rome's statesmen, but by the increase of the rabble and the consequent unmanageable character of her population, except under the firm hand of a single [Pg 126] master. And the reason why it took one hundred years of civil war to change the republic into the empire was not because the spirit of the republic was so slow in dying that its death struggles filled a century, but merely because the republic died too easily and the way to one-man power was so simple that there were too many candidates for the position, and hence the civil wars between them. These civil wars were bound to continue until the bitter lessons of experience had taught men not only how to gain the supreme control, which was relatively easy, but how to keep it and exclude rivals, which was much more difficult. The ambitious leaders of this century did not have to create a throne; that was ready to their hand. Their task was only to put defences around it. Even these defences of it were not directly against the people, for the people had no desire to overthrow the throne, but merely against the rival candidates. Step by step from Tiberius Gracchus to Gaius Gracchus, and on to Marius, to Sulla, to Pompey, to Julius Caesar, possession became more and more permanent; until from being a mere momentary position, it became nine points of the law, and Octavian made the tenure perfect by adding an almost religious reverence to his person in the title *Augustus*.

In the main the foreign wars of the second century before Christ gave place to the Civil War at home, but there was one exception to this, the war [Pg 127] with Mithradates, king of Pontus, which on various occasions during the early part of the century took large bodies of Romans to the Orient. And as though to supplement this knowledge of the East, in the closing half of the century the field of the civil struggle was enlarged so that it too included the East and South-East. We have already seen so many instances of the effects of political events on the course of Roman religion that it is a matter of no surprise to us to see that both of these struggles, the Civil War and the Oriental wars, left their marks on religion. It would be much more surprising if they had not done so. In the struggle of the rivals at home every possible weapon was employed, and it was soon discovered that the priests and the paraphernalia of religion were excellent means of political power and influence. The religion of the state therefore became enslaved to politics. On the other hand the campaigns in the East made the soldiers, and eventually on their return the whole populace, acquainted with various Oriental deities, which helped to satisfy their craving for the sensational and the superstitious. Thus while the state religion in its debauched condition was losing influence, the orgiastic element in worship was gaining power through these newly acquired Oriental cults. The story of the religion of the last century of the republic is accordingly the history of the control of state religion by politics and its consequent destruction, [Pg 128] and the growth of superstition because of the coming of new Oriental worships; and we may add to these two topics a third: the pathetic attempts of philosophy to breathe new life into the dead religion of the state.

When it comes to the question of the human characters whose names are writ large on this page of religious history, the Dictator Lucius Cornelius Sulla towers above all others. To his political insight is largely owing the harnessing of the state religion to the chariot of the politician, now and hereafter; and it was he who was the foremost leader of Roman armies to the Orient, and the man who, because of his peculiarly superstitious character, encouraged the worship of the strange deities which were found there. In both these directions he was ably seconded by Pompey, half a generation later. On the other hand the futile efforts of philosophy to improve the situation were inspired during the earlier period by the chief priest Scaevola, a contemporary of Sulla, and during Pompey's and Caesar's time by Varro, the greatest scholar that Rome ever produced.

Let us follow first the fortunes of the religion of the state at the hands of the politicians. The upper and influential classes of Roman society were now thoroughly imbued with Stoic philosophy and accordingly with the doctrine of the "double truth" in the field of religion—the real philosophical truth [Pg 129] which was their own peculiar property and which showed them clearly that all the forms of religion were vain, and its doctrines at best a clumsy statement in roundabout parables of a truth which they saw face to face; and that lower "truth" intended for the masses and dictated by the pressure of necessity, the concrete state religion in all its details, which must be preserved among the lower classes in the interest of the state and of society. The state religion was thus a matter of expediency and of usefulness. But once this idea of its usefulness was put into the foreground, it was natural that the question should immediately be asked: Was this state religion as useful after all as it might be? Could it not be put to greater uses? If religion existed in general for its political effects, why should it not be used by the individual, like any other political apparatus, for his own individual advancement? The man to whom this idea seems to have come first in all its fullness was Sulla, and he proceeded immediately to act upon it. The control of religion could, of course, be obtained best through the priesthoods, and those priesthoods were naturally most worth gaining which possessed the greatest right of interference in affairs of state. These priesthoods were: first the Augurs, with their traditional right to break up assemblies and to declare legislative action null and void; then the Pontiffs, with their general control of all vexed [Pg 130] questions concerning the intersection of divine and human law; and lastly the XVviri, or the keepers of the Sibylline books, in charge also of the cults to which the oracles had given birth. Accordingly he increased the numbers of these three priesthoods, raising each to fifteen; and inasmuch as the old right of the colleges of the priests to fill vacancies in their own bodies themselves had been taken away from them in B.C. 103, and such vacancies were now filled by popular vote, it was an easy thing for him to fill the new positions with his own men.

The result of accentuating the political importance of these three colleges was that the whole body of the state religion became actuated with a political spirit, and the whole structure was remodelled along the lines of this new valuation. The immediate effect of this was that the priests themselves became entirely absorbed in politics. To be sure Sulla was not responsible for all of this, because the tendency had been in this direction ever since the time of the Punic wars. In the good old days of Roman religion the office of priest had been in the main its own reward, and though the priests formed by no means a separate class, and the individual priest had many secular interests and occasionally some political ones, he was not supposed to hold political office. In the time of the Punic wars, however, the tide began to turn. The earliest recorded instance of a priest holding a [Pg 131] high political office is in the year B.C. 242 when the Flamen Martialis or special priest of Mars was chosen Consul; but when the gentleman in question started to go to the war, he was forbidden by the Pontifex Maximus. In B.C. 200 the Flamen Dialis, or special priest of Juppiter, was allowed to be made aedile, but his brother had to be especially authorised to take the oath of office in his stead, since the priest of Juppiter, the god of oaths, was himself not allowed to take an oath. In the course of the next century such cases became more common, and where the thing was not allowed, the priesthood became unpopular, and was sometimes left entirely vacant. This last thing happened, for instance, in the case of the Flaminium Diale, a position which was unfilled from B.C. 87 till B.C. 11. But the evil effects of politics were not confined to the emptying of certain priesthoods, which after all were of no very great importance, except as their presence tended to sustain the *morale* of the old religious ritual. Its effects were much more disastrous in the very important priesthoods which had now become essentially political offices. The exclusively political interests of the incumbents, combined with the fact that each man was elected by general vote of the people and without any special fitness for the position, as had been the case in the old days, tended to break down all the traditions of the college, and thus to destroy much [Pg 132] of the knowledge which was being handed down largely by oral tradition. There arose therefore an ignorance of the ritual of the cult which was great just in proportion as the knowledge originally present had been accurate and intricate. But even this was not all; the arranging of the yearly calendar, with its complicated intercalation of days to bring into harmony the solar and the lunar years, was still in the hands of the priests, and here the results of their growing ignorance were most appalling. The calendar became terribly disordered; and this again had its reaction on religion, for the calendar month occasionally fell so out of gear with the natural seasons that it was impossible to celebrate some of the old Roman festivals, which had a distinct bearing on certain seasons of the year.

Thus the greatest enemies of the religion of the state were those of its own household, the priests, who turned the reverent formalism of the old days into a mockery, and made their priesthood merely a means of political influence.

Now that the old Roman gods had been changed into new-fangled Greek gods, and the old Roman priesthoods into modern political clubs, it is little wonder that the religion of the fathers ceased to satisfy their descendants. But while history shows that specific religious creeds have often proved mortal and subject to change and decay, the same history makes clear that the religious instinct is a [Pg 133] constant factor in humanity; and we must not suppose for a moment that the religious need of the Roman community had ceased to exist, simply because the religion of the state had ceased to satisfy it. From the day when the Sibyl gave her first oracles to Rome on down to the time of Sulla, the desire for the sensational and the extraordinary in religion had been steadily growing. It had its birth in the idea that there was such a thing as a direct communion with the deity, and that the oracles were an immediate command from him. It was nourished by the sense of foreignness in the Greek ceremonies gradually introduced into the cult. It fed on the more sensational aspects of certain of the gods brought in: on the enthusiastic rites of Bacchus, on the miracle-working of Aesculapius, on the Stygian mystery of Dis and Proserpina. But its fulfilment was to come from the East, that inexhaustible fountain of religious energy. In the Magna Mater it recognised its own. This was the first undiluted Orientalism which came to Rome. But the state itself had received it, and had managed in some unaccountable way to put upon this outlandish Eastern cult the stamp of Rome's nationality, that stamp which no nation ever successfully and permanently resisted; and thus the reception of the cult on the part of the state was not only a disgraceful thing, tending to degrade true religion and spread the contagion of Orientalism, [Pg 134] but it also made those whose appetite had been aroused eager for other deities, whose cult would have the great additional charm of being unlicensed by the state, and hence savouring of unlawfulness.

Such a cult, long half-consciously desired, was at length found, when in B.C. 92 the Roman soldiery commanded by Sulla penetrated into the valley of Comana in Cappadocia. There was a whole community, a miniature state, devoted to the service of a goddess not unlike the Great Mother of Pessinus, but whose cult was more ecstatic, more orgiastic, than that of the Magna Mater, at least as Rome knew her. The king was the chief priest, and the citizens were priests and priestesses. The war with Mithradates brought the Roman army there again and also to another Comana in Pontus, where there was a branch of the Cappadocian cult. It was not the ignorant soldiery alone who were impressed by what they saw; their leader, Sulla, was fully as much affected, and on his return to Italy when the great crisis in his career, his march on Rome and his storming of the Eternal City, lay before him, it was the goddess of Comana who appeared to him in a dream and gave him courage. Thus her cult entered Rome, and the capture of the city by Sulla has its parallel in the capture of the hearts of the people by his companion, the goddess of Comana. The original name of this goddess seems to have been Mâ, but the Greeks, who also [Pg 135] knew her, had likened her to Enyo, their goddess of strife and warfare; hence in these days of facile identification the Romans' course was clear, and she became straightway Bellona, called by the name of their old goddess of war. Of all the chapters of the history of such identifications none is more curious than this. The old Bellona had borne to Mars the same relation that Fides, the goddess of good faith, had borne to

Juppiter. She was the result of the separate deification of one of the qualities of Mars, the breaking off of an adjective and the turning of it into a noun; but from now on, though the old goddess still existed and had her own temple and her own worship, the name was also applied to this strange Oriental goddess who came in the train of the debauched Roman army on its return from the East. But though men might call this new-comer by the name of a sacred old national goddess and worship her in private as they pleased, the religion of the state, even in its sunken condition, refused to admit her among its deities, and the priests, the *Fanatici*, with their wild dances, to the music of cymbals and trumpets, slashing themselves with their double axes until their arms streamed with blood, were not, at least as yet, the official representatives of the state, the companions of the reverend old Salii with their dignified "three-step." Even the sanctuaries of the private cult must be kept outside the city, and the violation of this law in B.C. 48 resulted [Pg 136] in the raiding and destruction of one of these private chapels. Her cult does not seem to have become a state affair until the beginning of the third century A.D., when Caracalla, who had extended Roman citizenship to all the inhabitants of the provinces, gave a similar citizenship to all the foreign deities resident in Rome. It is a curious coincidence that this action of Caracalla's occurred just about the same year A.D. in which the breakdown of the *pomerium* for state cults had occurred B.C. For the present, however, that is to say in the first century B.C., the state retained her dignity, though the resultant unorthodox character of the cult increased its power and influence, and made it more subversive to morals than the Magna Mater was.

An even more interesting instance, both of the popularity of sensational foreign cults and of the struggle of the state religion against them, is found in the case of the Egyptian goddess Isis. The spread of Isis worship into the Greek, and consequently also into the Roman world, began relatively early. In the third century Isis and her companion Serapis were well established on the island of Delos; and in the second century we find traces of their worship in Campania, especially at Pompeii and Puteoli. This last-named place, the seaport Puteoli, the modern Pozzuoli, outside of Naples, was probably the door through which Isis and her train came into Italy. Puteoli was the chief port [Pg 137] for Oriental ships, including Egypt, and it also had commercial relations with Delos. At this later date it supplied Rome with gods in somewhat the same way that Cumae, in the same neighbourhood, had done centuries before. So far as the city of Rome itself is concerned, an apparently trustworthy tradition traces the private cult back to the time of Sulla; and it certainly cannot have been introduced much later than this time, because in B.C. 58 it had became so prominent and so offensive to the authorities of the state that they destroyed an altar of Isis on the Capitoline. Apparently Isis was no exception to the general law of growth by persecution, because in the course of the next decade the state found it necessary to interfere no less than three times, *i.e.* in B.C. 53, 50, and 48. Finally the policy of suppression proved so ineffectual that it was decided to try the opposite extreme, and to see what could be done by state acknowledgment and state control, and so the Triumvirs, Octavian, Antony, and Lepidus, in B.C. 43 decreed the building of a state temple for Isis. But although they had decreed the erection of a temple, they were too much engaged in their own affairs to build it immediately, and until the temple was built Isis could not properly be considered among the state gods. As events turned out this temple was never built, for in the course of the next few years the trouble with Antony and Cleopatra began, and thus the gods [Pg 138] of Egypt became the gods of Rome's enemies, and so far as the state was concerned an acknowledgment of these gods was impossible. Instead Augustus forbade even private chapels inside the *pomerium*. The subsequent history of Isis does not directly concern us; suffice it to say that after various vicissitudes she was admitted to the state cult by Caracalla along with all the other foreign deities.

But it was not only Asia Minor and Egypt which gave their cults to Rome; the deities of Syria came too. Prominent among them was Atargatis, whose cult seems to have touched the Italian mainland first at Puteoli. In B.C. 54 the army of Crassus on its Eastern expedition, which was destined to come to such a tragic end in the terrible defeat at Carrhae, visited and plundered the sanctuary of the goddess in Syria. Thus she became known at Rome, where she was called simply the "Syrian goddess" (*dea Syria*) and was worshipped in a way very similar to the Magna Mater and Bellona.

Lastly when Pompey swept the Mediterranean clean of Cilician pirates, the sailors became acquainted with a Persian deity, Mithras, whose cult in Rome began during our period and subsequently crowded all the other orgiastic cults into insignificance.

We have now seen how the politicians were turning the state religion into a tool for the accomplishment of their own selfish ends, and how the masses [Pg 139] of the people were seeking satisfaction for their religious needs in sensational foreign worships, introduced from Asia Minor, Egypt, Syria, and Persia. We must now see whether any efforts were being made by any members of the community in behalf of the old religion, and whether there were still in existence any traces of the pure old Roman worship.

The latter-day philosophies of Greece had dealt a severe blow at Roman religion by convincing the intellectual classes in the community that in the nature of things there could be no such knowledge as that upon which religion was based, and hence that religion was an idle thing unworthy of a true man's interest. Yet all the philosophy in the world could not take away from a Roman his sense of duty to the state. Now the state in its experience had found religion so necessary that she had built up a formal system of it and made it a part of herself. As it was the duty of the citizen to support the state in every part of her activity, it was clearly his duty to support the state religion. Hence there arose that crass contradiction, which existed in Rome to a large degree as long as these particular systems of philosophy prevailed, between the duty which a man, as a thinking man, owed to himself, and the duty which he, as a good citizen, owed to the state. We have seen how during the second century before Christ no attempt was made to reconcile these two [Pg 140] views and how they existed side by side in such a man, for example, as Ennius, who wrote certain treatises embodying the most extraordinary sceptical doctrines, and certain patriotic poems in which the whole apparatus of the Roman gods is prominently exhibited and most reverently treated. We have also seen how this "double truth" could not but have disastrous results on the state religion in spite of all efforts to the contrary. The first effort which was made to improve the situation was not so much an attempt at reconciliation as a frank statement of the difficulties of the case. The problem had advanced considerably toward solution when once it had been clearly stated. The man who had the courage to make the statement was Quintus Mucius Scaevola, a famous lawyer as well as the head of the college of Pontiffs (Pontifex Maximus). He was a contemporary of Sulla, and was admirably fitted for his task because he not only represented religion in his position as Pontifex Maximus, but could speak also in behalf of the state both theoretically as a lawyer, and practically because he had filled almost all the important political offices (consul, B.C. 95). The treatise in which he made his statements has been lost to us, but we may obtain a fair idea of what he said from a quotation by the Christian writer Augustine in his wonderful book *The City of God* (iv. 27). For Scaevola the double truth of Ennius has grown into a triple truth, and there [Pg 141] are no less than three distinct religions: the religion of poets, of philosophers, and of statesmen. The religion of the poets, by which he means the mythological treatment of the gods, he condemns as worthless because it tells a great many things about the gods which are not true and which are entirely unworthy of them. The religion of philosophers he does not consider suitable to the state, because it contains many things which are superfluous, and some which are injurious. The superfluous things may be allowed to pass, but the injurious things, by which he evidently means the doctrines of Euhemeros, are a very serious matter, not because they are untrue but because the knowledge of them is inexpedient for the masses. The religion of the statesman can have no part in these things, even if they are true; and a man as a citizen of the state must believe in many things, or profess belief in them, which the same man, as an individual and a philosopher, knows are false. Scaevola's honest well-intentioned effort to support the religion of the state was naturally a failure. The very "masses" in whose behalf Scaevola was calling on his fellow-citizens to undergo these casuistical gymnastics soon cared more for Bellona and Isis than for all the gods of Numa together. But we cannot help admiring Scaevola for his patriotism, though we may not envy him his ethics. The state religion could never be supported on the arguments of expediency; [Pg 142] every one granted its expediency, and still it fell; its worst enemies, the politicians, granted it most of all, and they were the only ones who put the doctrine to any practical use. It was precisely this discovery of its expediency and its great practical value which caused its downfall. From the practical standpoint the problem was settled once and for all, but as a matter of theory it remained for the next generation, in the person of Varro, to provide a more satisfactory solution, and to effect something of a compromise between the truth of philosophy and the truth of religion.

Marcus Terentius Varro came to the work equipped with all the learning of his time and possessed of a greater knowledge of facts than any other Roman of his or any other day. So far as the problem of religion was concerned, he embodied this learning in the sixteen books of *Divine Antiquities*, which he very appropriately dedicated to Julius Caesar in his capacity as Pontifex Maximus. If Ennius's *Sacra Historia* be left out of account, his book was the first treatise on systematic theology which Rome ever had. In this work he desired to accomplish three things: first, by a review of the history of Rome to show how essential the state religion was; second, by an examination of Greek mythology to purify the state religion from its immoral influences; third, to show that the state religion so purified was fully in accord with Stoic [Pg 143] philosophy. In regard to the "three religions," therefore, he agreed with Scaevola in casting out entirely the religion of the poets, and in accepting both the others, but he differed from Scaevola in that he denied the contradiction between them and asserted that they were not two truths but two forms of the same truth. We are not able to go into the details of his attempt, because unfortunately the books in which he wrote it have been lost to us, and we have again merely the quotation in Augustine's *City of God*. But we know that in general he tried to show that the formal doctrines of the state religion were merely a popular presentation of the truths of the Stoic philosophy, and that the whole system of Roman gods could be reduced in theory to the great philosophical contrast between the sky and the earth, the procreative and the conceptive elements. A man might therefore hold fast to both religions as to a simpler creed and a more abstruse one. Hence a man's belief as a good citizen and his belief as an intelligent individual were not in contrast so far as the truth was concerned, but merely in the matter of form, in the manner of presentation. Varro's heroic effort, supported as it was by all the learning of his day and all the influence that his fame lent to his words, was nevertheless a failure. The religion of the state was dead; politics had killed it. It was a political power alone which could restore life to it, but that was [Pg 144] the work of an emperor, Augustus, and not of a scholar, Varro.

While Varro, with the weapon of philosophy, was attempting to defend the religion of the state against its enemies, the poets and the philosophers, a poet, also armed with philosophy, was trying to defend the Roman people against its worst enemy, superstition. It may not seem as though Lucretius belonged among the friends of old Roman religion, and as though the *De Rerum Natura* were exactly a religious poem, and yet his work was in so far helpful to old Roman religion in that it attacked the excesses of a latter-day superstition which had alienated the hearts of the people from their old beliefs. Superstition is a parasite which lives on scepticism, and with the killing of the parasite scepticism sometimes dies as well; and it is open to question whether Lucretius's book was not of considerable service in the cause of religion. For religion still lived at Rome, though it is the fashion of the writers on the ethics of the close of the republic to emphasise almost entirely the scepticism of the day, dwelling on the attitude of a Cicero or a Caesar, and forgetting the infinite number of "little people," especially outside of Rome in the country, who still believed in the old religion of the fathers, and who still performed the old festivals of Numa, people who knew no more about Isis than they did about Stoic philosophy. Their presence is disclosed [Pg 145] to us in a few republican inscriptions, but better yet in the continuance of the rites of family worship down into the latest days of Rome, rites which did not form a part of the restoration of Augustus, and which therefore, had they died now, would never have come to life again. It is by just so much more our duty to remember these people, as they have been forgotten by history, if we ever expect to obtain a picture of Roman religion in its true proportions. They were besides the people upon whom Augustus built in the restoration, to which we now turn.

[Pg 146]

THE AUGUSTAN RENAISSANCE

Politics had caused the downfall of the state religion. Weakened by the attacks of a sceptical philosophy, driven from the hearts of the common people by the rival cults of the Orient, the state religion had finally lost all its influence by the abuse of it as a political tool. Its priesthoods were deserted, its temples were falling into ruins with the grass carpeting their mosaic pavements and the spiders weaving new altar cloths. To us with our modern ideas it would have seemed impossible that this state religion could ever rise again; and probably no other state religion that the world has ever seen could have been brought to life again, because no other state religion has ever been so absolutely a part of the state, unless the state itself were a theocracy; and possibly no lesser genius than Augustus could have accomplished the task even under the slightly more favourable conditions which the state religion of Rome offered. Whether Julius Caesar would have attempted the restoration is one of the many questions which his death left [Pg 147] unanswered. Certainly thoughtful men of his day hoped that he would, and it was in this hope that Varro dedicated his *Divine Antiquities* to him; and another contemporary, Granius Flaccus, his book *On the Invocation of the Gods*. But except for one law which he caused to be enacted "concerning the priesthoods," we have no knowledge either of his accomplishment or of his intentions, and the great task was left practically untouched for the master-hand of Augustus.

In order that we may understand what Augustus did and how he managed to succeed in relation to the state religion we must obtain some idea of the whole scheme of Augustus in relation to the state at large, of which his religious reorganisation was merely a part. One of the cleverest characterisations of the Emperor Augustus which has ever been written was that by the late Professor Mommsen, but its relatively secluded position in the Latin preface to an edition of Augustus's great autobiography, the *Res Gestae*, has prevented it from being generally known. Mommsen describes Augustus as "a man who wore most skilfully the mask of a great man, though himself not great." This epigrammatic statement is undoubtedly clever but it is not just, although it is the opinion concerning Augustus which we would expect a man to hold who, like Mommsen, had an almost unbounded admiration for Julius Caesar. There have been [Pg 148] scattered through the pages of history even down to our own day men of whom we say that they were not great men, though they did a great work. In certain cases doubtless we can separate the man from his work and justify the assertion, but in other cases we are deceived by the man himself just as his contemporaries were and as he wished them to be. For it occasionally happens that a man who is called to rule over men and to reorganise a disordered government is able best to accomplish his end by a gentle diplomacy, a conciliatory manner, which is often misunderstood by those who surround him and who interpret gentleness of spirit as smallness of spirit and self-restraint as weakness. It would be truer to describe Augustus as a man who wore most skilfully the mask of an ordinary man though himself an extraordinary man. The more we study the chaotic condition of Rome under the Second Triumvirate and the more fully we realise not only the total disorganisation of the forms of government but also the absolute demoralisation of the individual citizen, the more we appreciate the almost impossible task which was set for Augustus and which he successfully accomplished. For one hundred years (B.C. 133-31), from Tiberius Gracchus to Actium, hardly a decade had passed which had not brought forth some terrible revolution for Rome. Even the great Caesar had failed, had not divined aright the only treatment to which the disease of the [Pg 149] age would yield, for although the blows which actually killed Caesar may have been merely an accident in history, the deed of irresponsible men, his fall was no accident but was the inevitable logical outcome of his imperial policy. But Augustus succeeded in establishing a form of government which enabled himself and his connexion to occupy the throne for almost a hundred years, and even then though revolutions came, his constitution was the main bulwark of government in succeeding centuries. It would take us too far from our present subject to answer in any completeness the question of how he succeeded, but a word or two may be said in general, and the rest will become clearer when we examine his reorganisation of religion.

The secret of Augustus's success was the infinite tact and diplomacy by which he managed to strengthen the throne and his own position on it while apparently restoring the form of the republic and the manners of the old days. It is open to question whether he was actuated by a consideration of the good of the state, or by a regard for his own selfish ends, but it is beyond question that he gave to Rome the only form of government which could eradicate the habit of revolution, and thus saved the state. He succeeded because he did not underestimate the difficulty of the task, and accordingly brought to bear on it every possible influence, emphasising especially the psychological element [Pg 150] and being willing to go a long way around in order to arrive at his goal. He was not content with a mere temporary makeshift, which might carry him to the end of his own life; he was laying foundations for the future. Nowhere is this more clearly stated than in one of his edicts, where he says: — "May it fall to my lot to establish the state firm and strong and to obtain the wished-for fruit of my labours, that I may be called the author of it and that when I die I may carry with me the hope that the foundations which I have laid may abide." These abiding foundations must be laid deep in the national psychology, and it was his grasp of the psychological problem which explains his reorganisation of religion. A century of civil war had totally destroyed the spirit of unity and created an infinite number of petty hatreds between man and man. Men had looked so long at their individual interests that they had almost forgotten the existence of the state. But if the spirit of patriotism could be quickened into a new life, then men would think of the state and forget themselves, and united in their love of this one universal object of devotion they would learn a lesson of union which might gradually be extended to their whole life. But the state must be presented not as it was in all its wretchedness, lacerated by civil struggle; the sight of the present would serve only to start the quarrel over again; instead it must be the ideal state, a [Pg 151] state so far away, so distant from all the citizens, that they all seemed equally near. If this state were to be something more than a mere abstraction, it could be clothed only in the reverential garments of the past, it must be the Rome of the good old days. Yet if they were not for ever to mourn a "Golden Age" in the past and a paradise that was lost, there must also be a hope for the future, a paradise to be regained. In a word the belief in the eternity of Rome must be instilled into men's hearts. Thus was the idea of the "eternal city" born, and it is no mere coincidence that the first instance of this phrase in literature occurs in Tibullus, a poet of the Augustan age. Once convinced of the eternity of Rome men could look at the past for inspiration in full confidence that the beauties which had been could be obtained again. But Augustus was more than a sentimental enthusiast, and he saw that it was not enough for men to drop their swords at the epiphany of "Roma

Aeterna," that their eyes would grow weary and looking to earth would behold the swords again. These swords must be beaten into ploughshares and pruning hooks; the deserted farms of Italy must be filled again, and the stability of the state must be increased by an enlargement of the agricultural community. But for the accomplishment of these reforms something was needed which was at once gentler and stronger than legal [Pg 152] enactments. The poet must make smooth the way of the law. It was the poet who could best interest men in the past; and thus Augustan poetry was encouraged and directed by the emperor, that by pointing out the glories of old Rome it might inspire men to make a new Rome more glorious than the old. Practically every poet of the age was directly or indirectly under the influence of the ruler. It was the emperor's counsellor, Maecenas, who encouraged Virgil to write his *Georgics*, and these glowing pictures of farm life did quite as much to carry out the emperor's plans as the *Aeneid* later. And Virgil was not alone in writing of country life; Tibullus, even more gentle than the gentle bard of Mantua, was telling the same story in another form.

By this time the myths which Greece had given to Rome or which Rome had made for herself on Greek models were absolutely a part of the national past. These too entered into Augustus's scheme. Thus another protégé of Maecenas, the poet Propertius, was gradually weaned from love poetry and filled instead with a hunger for the myths of Roman temples and of old Roman customs, so that Cynthia slowly gives way to Tarpeia and Vertumnus, and the Rome of Augustus to the Rome of Romulus. Even the irrepressible Ovid tried in his exuberant fashion to assist in this work and started in his *Fasti* to write a history of the [Pg 153] religious festivals of the Roman year. But above all these, and infinitely more important in its influence, towers the *Aeneid* of Virgil. All through the varied incidents of the twelve books there runs the scarlet thread of a great purpose, the glorification of Rome and of Augustus. From the sack of Troy, through the long wanderings and the fierce wars in Latium, down to the final conquest of the enemy, we see Aeneas led by the hand of the gods whose will it was that Rome should be. The lesson is very evident. The providence which guided us in the past still protects us; we have no right to be discouraged, and our future is assured us under the same gods who brought our fathers out of the land of the Trojans, through the midst of the Greeks. But there is concealed in the *Aeneid* another lesson, much more directly useful to Augustus. Its hero, the immaculate pious Aeneas, is the direct ancestor of the Julian house to which Augustus belongs, and the founding of Rome shows not only the good will of the gods toward the city, but in no less degree their special appointment and protection of the leader. The descendants of the house of Aeneas are therefore the divinely appointed rulers of Rome.

There can be no question but that this poetry had an effect none the less far reaching because its influence was difficult to estimate and analyse. It was not necessary for the psychological result that [Pg 154] men should actually believe in these myths; much was gained if they allowed their thoughts to dwell on the ideas presented in them. It was the sedimentary deposit thus formed which was to fertilise the soil of patriotism which had grown so barren in the civil wars. But while Augustus was broad-minded enough to realise the value of the influence of literature, he did not fail to recognise that men could not live by myths alone, that they must be surrounded by visible cult acts and tangible temples of the gods in order that their faith might be aided by sight and their life filled with action. Literature was to encourage patriotism, and patriotism was the foundation for the spiritual restoration of the state religion, but the state itself must by legal enactment prepare the outward form which the religious activity was to take. The question of the sincerity of Augustus in these religious reforms is a very difficult one to answer. If the essence of religion consisted in acts and not in belief, in works and not in faith, Augustus was a devoutly religious man. Beyond that we cannot go, for our judgment is hampered not only by ignorance of the facts but by our inability to free ourselves from the modern standpoint in the interpretation of the few facts that we do know. There can be no question of the emperor's fitness for the task so far as priestly learning went, for he was from a very early age a member of three priesthoods: a pontiff, an augur, [Pg 155] and a guardian of the Sibylline books. With characteristic modesty however he refrained from becoming Chief Pontiff until in B.C. 12 the death of Lepidus, the discarded member of the Second Triumvirate, left the position vacant.

One who understands the political reforms of Augustus will have no difficulty in understanding his reorganisation of religion, for they were both undertaken with the same general underlying principles and along similar lines. In both cases innovations and novelties were strenuously avoided, except of course those of a merely administrative character. In each case a successful effort was made to have it appear as if the old institutions of the republic were being reinstated, whereas as a matter of fact the form alone was old with its age artificially emphasised occasionally by an archaistic touch, while the content was quite new. The real result in each case was the strengthening of the monarchy and the emphasising of the divine right of the Julian house. In our study of Augustus's restoration of religion we must not be content therefore with chronicling the old forms which were re-established, but we must examine in each case the new content which was put into them, even though the evidence of that content consists oftentimes of a mere tendency. The fondness of Augustus for the archaic is nowhere more clearly exhibited than in one of his earliest religious acts: the formal declaration [Pg 156] of war against Antony and Cleopatra, in B.C. 32, by means of the Fetiales. The Fetiales were a very ancient priestly college which acted, under the direction of the Senate, as the representatives of international law. It was through them that all treaties and all declarations of war had been made, but it seems probable that this custom had fallen into desuetude after the Punic wars, and that accordingly the college had lapsed into insignificance, if it had not died out altogether. But now as the first step in the rebuilding of the priesthoods Octavian restored the college to its old rank and gained also the additional advantage that the people were impressed with the moral righteousness of their cause against Antony and Cleopatra, and also with the fact that it was a foreign, *i.e.* an international war, and not a civil one, in which they were about to engage. The effect of Octavian's restoration was a lasting one, for from this time on this priesthood was held in high honour during the whole of the empire, and the emperors themselves were members of it.

This was a very characteristic beginning to Augustus's activity. It was primarily the human element to which he was appealing in his religious changes, and hence the priesthoods needed especial attention. It was not long after the battle of Actium that he restored another very ancient priesthood, that of the Arval brothers. This was a very [Pg 157] old priesthood consisting of twelve men who took part in the purification of the land, the *Ambarvalia*, so called because the ceremony consisted of a solemn procession around the boundaries of the fields. But as the Roman territory grew and such a ceremony in the old fashion became impossible and was carried out merely symbolically by sacrifices at various boundary points, the Arval brothers lost all their importance, so that even in these symbolic sacrifices their place was taken by the pontiffs. Augustus however recognised in this priesthood an effectual means of emphasising the agricultural side of Roman life, and of connecting the imperial family with the farming population. The centre of this new worship was the sanctuary in the sacred grove at the fifth milestone of the Via Campana, and it is there that the wonderful discoveries have been made of the inscriptions giving the "minutes" of the meetings of this curious corporation, beginning with Augustus. But the pastoral side of their worship was an insignificant matter, even in the age of Augustus, compared with their prayers and supplications in behalf of the imperial house, so that the records of this supposedly agricultural priesthood form one of our best sources for the study of emperor-worship.

Three other priesthoods, the pontiffs, the augurs, and the guardians of the Sibylline books (*XVviri*) did not need actual restoration, for their ability [Pg 158] to interfere in politics had kept them alive during the closing centuries of the republic, when political usefulness was the surest means of surviving in the struggle for existence. But the fact that they had been politically powerful made the control of them all the more necessary for an emperor who wished to have in his hands all the possibilities of political influence. It was contrary to Augustus's policy openly to crush any of the institutions which had really been or, what was from his standpoint very much the same thing, had been thought to be a bulwark of republicanism. As a matter of fact however these priesthoods had been one of the chief means of bringing the republic into the control of one man. Hence for Augustus the problem was easy to solve; it was only necessary to appear to honour these priesthoods by raising their dignity still higher and by making only men of senatorial rank eligible, and then to take the chief position in them himself and to fill them with his own supporters. Thus the republic was apparently saved and the empire was really strengthened.

But the priesthood to which Augustus devoted his most especial attention was the priesthood of Vesta, the Vestal virgins. Here he was guided not only by his desire to improve the condition of the priesthoods in general but also by his especial interest in the cult of Vesta. The reasons for this interest in Vesta will be explained in a moment when we [Pg 159] discuss the emperor's favourite cults; but a word about its effects on the priestesses of Vesta may be said here. The Vestal virgins had been relatively little contaminated by politics, but the priesthood had suffered along with all the rest of the religion of the state because of the general indifferentism and neglect of religious things which characterised the closing centuries of the republic. The best families in the state were not as ready as in the earlier days to devote their daughters to the service, and thus the rank and consequently the influence of the Vestals had to some extent declined. But now all this was immediately changed, the outward honour and the insignia of the Vestals were increased until they were allowed such privileges as not even the emperors possessed. When they went through the street, they were attended by a lictor as the higher officers of the state were, and they were given special seats at the theatre. But the most characteristic thing which Augustus did for them and that which helped their cause the most was the emperor's declaration, made to be repeated in public gossip, that if he had a grand-daughter of the proper age he would unhesitatingly make her a Vestal virgin.

Toward the close of his life Augustus prepared a statement of what he had accomplished during his reign, a sort of *compte rendu* of his stewardship. In a roundabout way almost all of this has been preserved to us and it naturally forms the [Pg 160] greatest source of our knowledge of his activity. After reciting a large number of his religious reforms he adds:—"The spoils of war I have consecrated to the gods in the Capitoline temple, in the temple of the god Julius, in the temple of Apollo, in the temple of Vesta, in the temple of Mars the Avenger." These words give us a clue to the more especial religious interests of Augustus, a clue which is all the more needed because of his apparently catholic spirit, and his seemingly general interest in all the forms of old Roman religion. No man who restored and in some cases entirely rebuilt eighty-two temples to various deities could be accused of undue partiality in emphasising certain phases of religion to the total exclusion of others. But as a matter of fact underneath this general interest there were present certain very specific interests, and this passage in his own writing adds great strength to the other evidence as to what these gods were. Naturally in every list of pre-eminent deities Juppiter must be present, hence the mention of the Capitoline temple first; as a matter of fact however Augustus's worship of Juppiter was much more a matter of form than of real interest. His attitude was one of graceful acceptance of the inevitable rather than of enthusiastic homage. Juppiter was not adapted to his purpose, because it was almost impossible to connect Juppiter with a specific form of government other than the republic, much less with a particular [Pg 161] royal family like the Julian house. Juppiter had come to mean republicanism. The Capitoline temple had ushered in the republic in B.C. 509 and there was a halo of republicanism about it which was too genuine to be used as a mask for concealing imperial features. With the four other deities matters stood very differently. The god Julius, Apollo, Vesta, and Mars the Avenger were either already identical with the imperial family or could easily be connected with it.

The central feature of the religion of the empire was a thing altogether unique and unknown in the republic: the worship of the emperors as gods. From Augustus on this was the chief characteristic of the state religion; its beginnings must be sought therefore under his reign and he is largely accountable for it. According to our modern ideas it seems a very strange thing to worship a living man as a god; it seems also strange to worship a dead man as a god, but there we have at least the analogy of the worship of the saints, and the inherent instinct of the race toward ancestor-worship which unexpectedly crops out in all of us at intervals. But we must rid ourselves of modern ideas and try to appreciate the historical evolution of emperor-worship. This evolution is perfectly clear and we can trace every step of it, though in doing so we must remember that the various processes which we are compelled to take up one after [Pg 162] another in our explanation went on in nature side by side, and exercised a sympathetic influence one upon the other, which we have to eliminate from our explanation but make allowance for in our finished concept.

We have seen that from the very beginning of religious life in Rome the idea was present that everything, each individual and each family, had its divine double, the individual in the shape of his Genius, the family in the shape of protecting spirits, Vesta, the Penates, and later the Lar. In addition to this, under the influence of the Greek myths which various families adopted, certain gods originally independent became especially associated with these families. Each family was naturally interested in the worship of its own gods, but this particular worship was quite as naturally confined to the particular family or its dependents. Now the first preliminary step toward emperor-worship was taken when the gods of the imperial family began to be worshipped by other families, then by all other families, and officially by the state. But from the very beginning the gods of each family had included also the deified ancestors, the *Di Manes,* at first thought of *en masse* and not as individuals, but toward the close of the republic they began to be individualised, so that the next step in emperor-worship was when the dead Julius, a particular ancestor therefore of Augustus, began to be wor [Pg 163] shipped by the whole people and officially by the state. But also from the beginning there had been still another element in family worship, the cult paid to the Genius or divine double of the living master of the house. There followed then correspondingly as another step toward emperor-worship, the homage paid by the whole state to the Genius of the living emperor. These three steps: the worship by the whole state of the gods of the emperor's family, in its three forms, the gods of the family in general, and in particular the deified ancestor, and the Genius of the living representative, were all encouraged and officially established by Augustus. Lastly there came from the Orient a habit of thought in distinct contradiction to Roman ideas whereby not the Genius of the living emperor but the very man himself was divine in life and in death. Augustus fought against this concept but had to yield to it and allow himself to be worshipped directly as a god in the Orient itself and in certain coast towns of Italy which were under strong Oriental influence, but he forbade it in Rome, and thus established a precedent which was followed by all the better ones among the emperors who came after him.

This digression was necessary in order that we might appreciate the reasons for Augustus's preferences in emphasising certain cults. Unquestionably he did not foresee or plan for an emperor-worship such as eventually grew up out of his arrangements; [Pg 164] he was however deeply interested in emphasising the worship of the special deities of his own family. The four gods therefore whose names he couples with that of Juppiter in the summary of his religious activity—Apollo, Vesta, Mars the Avenger, and the god Julius—are all intimately connected with his family; and if we add to this the worship of his own Genius, the Genius Augusti, we shall have the real kernel of his religious restoration. It remains for us to see in what way these deities are connected with his family, and how he managed to emphasise their cult and at the same time to bring them into close relationship to himself.

From the time of his first introduction into Rome Apollo had stood in a relation of contrast to Juppiter. Apollo's oracles, the Sibylline books, had brought in a host of Greek gods whose presence tended inevitably to lessen the unique position and the unparalleled prestige of Juppiter Optimus Maximus, the great representative of nationalism in Roman religion. At first this contrast was scarcely marked, and the very oracles of Apollo which were destined to undermine Juppiter's omnipotence were stored in Juppiter's temple and under his protection. The difference was felt more strongly as the priesthood of the Sibylline books began to grow in influence alongside of the pontiffs, the priests of the Juppiter cults. This opposition was emphasised in B.C. 367, when the priesthood of the oracles was opened to [Pg 165] the plebeians, while the pontiffs were still patricians. At first unquestionably the object of the patricians was to keep for themselves the more sacred and the then more important college and to open the lesser priesthood to the plebeians. But in the struggle of the two orders those things which were opened to the plebeians grew in importance and entirely overshadowed those which were so scrupulously hedged about, and the elements which strove to resist progress were crushed beneath it; and just as the old assembly, the Comitia Curiata, which the patricians had kept for themselves, was later of no account compared with the Comitia Centuriata, which belonged to both orders, so the college of pontiffs lost significance while the keepers of the oracles gained steadily in power and influence. But it was not merely because Apollo was the great leader of the Greek movement in Roman religion that Augustus chose to honour him. A far more important consideration guided him, for Apollo was especially attached to the Julian house in all its mythical and historical fortunes. The first great public evidence of Apollo's favour in Augustus's career was at the battle of Actium; but while this led to the first proclamation of the emperor's devotion to Apollo, it was not Actium which made him a worshipper of the god, but it was because he was a worshipper of Apollo from the beginning that Actium and all subsequent tokens of the god's favour were emphasised by him. [Pg 166] However much or little the people of the day may have known about Apollo's previous relations to the Julian family, the legend of his assistance at Actium, and the immortalisation of that legend in the great temple on the Palatine were proofs enough. The moral effect of the Palatine temple cannot be overestimated, especially when we realise one fact, which is often neglected, that this temple gained infinitely in significance because it was on private ground, attached to the emperor's own private house, for we must not forget that the Palatine was only in process of transition into the imperial residence, and though the house of Augustus, when he left it, was the palace, during his lifetime it was merely his private residence. The temple of Apollo was therefore in its origin theoretically the private chapel of a Roman family rather than the seat of a state cult. It was the Apollo of the Julian house who was being worshipped there. And yet it was far more than a private worship, for it began very soon to be a cult centre in distinct rivalry to Juppiter Optimus Maximus on the Capitoline. The oracles of the Sibyl, even though they were the words of Apollo, had never been preserved in the old temple of Apollo on the Flaminian meadow, but instead they had always been in the custody of Juppiter on the Capitoline. But now these oracles, after being carefully revised by the emperor, were deposited in the new Palatine temple, and by this [Pg 167] act the centre of all the Greek cults in Rome was transferred from Juppiter to Apollo, from the Capitoline to the Palatine, and the rivalry between the two was publicly declared. The temple was dedicated in B.C. 28 and Augustus allowed its influence to permeate the Roman people for more than a decade before he took the next step, a step which was virtually to parallel Apollo and his sister Artemis-Diana with Juppiter and Juno.

Among the Greek gods who came into Rome we saw the entrance in the middle of the third century before Christ of a pair of deities of the Lower World, Dis and Proserpina, and in connexion with the introduction the establishment of certain games called "secular" because they were to be repeated at the expiration of a century (*saeculum*). The initial celebration was in B.C. 249, one hundred years later with a slight delay they were celebrated again in B.C. 146, the next anniversary was omitted because it fell in the midst of the civil war between Caesar and Pompey, but now Augustus wished to celebrate them. There were chronological difficulties, but they did not prove insurmountable. An oracle was set in circulation, or one actually in circulation was made use of, wherein it was declared that a great cycle of four times one hundred and ten years had passed and that a new age was now beginning. The emperor, if not responsible for this oracle, was very willing to accept it. It was an essential part [Pg 168] of his plan that all things should become new, and that with the new age should come a new spirit. This new *saeculum* must be ushered in by games which should be at once like and unlike those of past centuries. They were to be celebrated at least in part on the hallowed spot, the *Tarentum* in the Campus Martius, they were to extend through three nights like the old games, but the three days were to be added as well, and the deities worshipped in the night, while they were no longer the old gods of the Lower World, Dis and Proserpina, were at least mysterious deities of fate and fortune, while the gods of the day, Apollo and Artemis, Juppiter and Juno, were as new to the games as the day celebrations themselves were. But the equality of Apollo and Juppiter was expressed not merely in the parallelisation of Juppiter-Juno with Apollo-Diana. It was still more in evidence on the third and greatest day of the festival, when the procession of three times nine youths and three times nine maidens sang the song in honour of Apollo and Diana, which Horace wrote and which has been preserved to us among his writings, the *Carmen Saeculare,* and to which in addition the recently found inscription giving an account of the games bears witness in the words *carmen composuit Q. Horatius Flaccus* (*C.I.L.* vi.

32323). On this day the procession started from the Apollo temple on the Palatine, and went over to the Juppiter temple [Pg 169] on the Capitoline, and then back again to Apollo on the Palatine, thus indicating not only the equality of Apollo and Juppiter but even the superiority of the former. A new age had indeed begun, an age in which the new associations of the Palatine and the glamour of imperialism were to overcome the more democratic associations of the Capitoline with its incorrigibly republican Juppiter. Greek gods which had hitherto in theory at least been subordinated to the gods of old Rome were now granted not only equality but superiority. The specific cult of Apollo, to be sure, did not always retain the exalted position to which Augustus had raised it, but even it never entirely lost its prominence, whereas the general idea of the supremacy of the imperial cult was now established for all time to come. But this secular celebration of Augustus is interesting aside from the relation of Juppiter and Apollo, for it affords another illustration of the skilful combination of new and old in the Augustan reorganisation. In form the festival is avowedly the old one, but in two respects at least it introduces a new element. In the first place participation in the old festival, as in all the old festivals, had been confined to Roman citizens. Others might look on, but they could not take part, nor were they the recipients of any of the blessings which were to follow. But now every free member of the community, with wife and child, might join [Pg 170] in the celebration, and thus the note was struck which was to be the keynote of all that was best in the changes introduced by the empire whose "highest and most beautiful task," as Professor Mommsen puts it, "and the one which she fulfilled most perfectly, was gradually to reconcile and thus to put an end to the contrast between the ruling city and the subordinate communities, and thus to change the old Roman law of city-citizenship into a community of the state which embraced all the members of the empire." But even this was not all; under the guise of this restoration of an old republican institution a blow was struck at the very foundation of all republican institutions, namely the power of the Senate. It was *par excellence* Augustus's festival, arranged by him or by those to whom he had committed the details. The Senate had little or nothing to say about it and yet the control of such religious celebrations had hitherto formed an inalienable part of the Senate's power. Even in the procession itself the republican magistrates do not seem to have been officially present. It was thus no longer the Senate inviting the magistrates and the citizens in good and regular standing to perform a certain divine function, but it was the emperor inviting all the members of the community, citizens and non-citizens alike, to join with him in worshipping the gods of the new state.

A great part of Augustus's success was un [Pg 171] questionably due to a certain form of moral courage. For all his diplomacy and his desire to feel the pulse of the people he was never lacking in the courage of his own convictions. This can be seen nowhere better than in his attitude toward his adoptive father Julius Caesar. From the very beginning when he took upon himself, even at the cost of temporary impoverishment, the payment of Caesar's legacy, he was supremely true to the man whose successor he was, and this faithfulness is especially apparent in the field of religion. Here there are two cults, both relating to Julius Caesar, for which Augustus was largely responsible, that of the god Julius himself, and that of Mars the Avenger.

In consideration of what Caesar had already done for the reorganisation of the state, and in view of what he was planning to carry out, his death was a national calamity, but his influence might still be rescued and preserved by elevating him into the rank of the gods. For the accomplishment of this it was necessary that the Senate should act, for in the hands of the Senate alone lay the power to receive new gods into the state. Thus the god Julius was created and the word *divus* received a new meaning. With that logic which was characteristic of Roman religion from the very beginning, the elevation of Julius into the ranks of the greater and more individual gods went side by side with his exclusion from the ranks of the ordinary deified ancestors, so [Pg 172] that thereafter at the funeral processions of the Julian family his wax mask was absent from the processions of ancestors to which he no longer belonged, but in the parade of the circus he was present, drawn in a waggon among the greater gods. Nothing was left undone to render his cult both conspicuous and permanent. A special priest (*flamen*) was appointed to look after it, and as the irony of fate would have it one of the first incumbents of this position was Marc Antony after his reconciliation with Augustus in B.C. 40. Then too a special festival day was given him among the religious holidays of the year. It was intended that this day should be July 13, his birthday, but as that day happened to be already devoted to an important celebration in connexion with the games of Apollo, the day preceding it, July 12, was chosen. But more was needed than a priest and a holiday, there must be a cult centre as well, a temple of the Divus Julius. The site of this temple was already given in the associations connected with Caesar's death. There could be but one place for it, and that was in the Forum near the Regia where his body had been carried to be burned. There the temple was built and dedicated August 18, B.C. 29. An altar had been erected on the spot where Caesar's body had been burned, and the new temple was so placed that the altar was included in its boundaries, occupying a niche in the centre of the front line of the substructure. The temple had the usual history [Pg 173] of destruction and rebuilding in antiquity until in early Christian times it was used for secular purposes, and the eyesore of the pagan altar was removed by building a wall across the front, the diameter of the semicircular niche, and by roofing the altar over on a level with the existing platform. Thus the altar with its historical and religious associations was entirely lost sight of, and though the temple in its main outlines had long been excavated, the altar was not discovered until 1898, when the wall was broken through and the whole thing laid bare. Thus by the vote of the Senate, the appointment of a priest, the setting apart of a holy day in the year, and the building of a temple, the worship of the god Julius was established; but it was the general irresistible tendency toward emperor-worship which kept it alive and made it the model for a tremendous subsequent development. Augustus had accomplished his desire. Men were looking on Caesar as a success after all and not as a failure. The *Di Manes* of a murdered emperor had been profitably exchanged for the Divus Julius, and just as the gods had founded the old Rome of Romulus, so again it was a god who had laid the foundations of the empire over which his successor was ruling.

But Augustus was not content with this; it was all very well for men to look upon the god Caesar as an illustration of justification after death, as an example of how heaven could right the wrongs of [Pg 174] earthly existence, but that was not sufficient; the punishment of those who caused his earthly downfall must be emphasised, it must be shown that the gods were quite as much interested in punishing the sinner as in rewarding the righteous man who was sinned against. It was one thing to transfer one's ancestors to the gods, it was quite another thing to take measures to keep oneself from following in their footsteps, even though their last estate was theoretically desirable. Hence side by side with the cult of the Divus Julius went that of Mars Ultor, Mars the Avenger. The circumstances of the beginning of the cult show that it was no mere poetical title but a genuine cult-name born in an earnest moment: for the great temple subsequently built to Mars under this cognomen was vowed by Augustus "in behalf of vengeance for his father," in the war against the slayers of Caesar, Brutus and Cassius. This temple, vowed at Philippi in B.C. 42, was so slow in building that in the meantime Augustus erected a small round temple to Mars Ultor on the Capitoline. This was dedicated May 12, B.C. 20. In the years which followed Augustus proceeded with the difficult and extremely expensive task of purchasing property for his own Forum, and here was built and dedicated, August 1, B.C. 2, the great temple of Mars Ultor. But aside from being a very present reminder of the vengeance which the gods had in store for those who killed a Caesar, it stood also for the Julian [Pg 175] house, for Mars was not alone in the temple but with him was Venus, the ancestral mother of the family of Julius and Augustus; and thus was once more emphasised the connexion between the ancestors of the ruling house and the great ancestor Mars, from whom all Romans were sprung.

A temple possessed of such strong associations with the imperial family became instantly a centre of their family worship, and in this respect produced another rival to the cult of Juppiter on the Capitoline. In connexion namely with the putting on of the *toga virilis* the members of the imperial family went to the temple of Mars Ultor instead of following the immemorial custom of ascending the Capitol to the shrine of Juppiter Optimus Maximus. More important yet the insignia of the triumph, which had always been in the keeping of the Capitoline Juppiter even before he was Optimus Maximus and while he was only the "Striker," Feretrius, were now preserved in the temple of Mars Ultor.

With all the state worshipping Apollo, the god of the emperor's own family, on the Palatine, celebrating the divinity of his ancestor the god Julius in the Roman Forum, and acknowledging Mars as the avenger of all those who did the emperor harm, in the emperor's own new Forum, it might have seemed to a less far-seeing man that religion had been sufficiently pressed into the service of the royal family. But so it did not seem to Augustus. These cults were [Pg 176] all three of them essentially new, and new cults may, to be sure, easily become prominent; they usually do, but the test comes with time whether there is external pressure sufficiently continuous to give permanency to this prominence. As a matter of fact not one of these three cults continued later to hold the rank in importance which it had under Augustus. On the other hand if one went low enough and looked sufficiently deep down certain elements in the religious life of the community could be found which continued almost unchanged from century to century. These were the simple elements which were involved in family worship, the sacrifices at the hearth of Vesta, and those to the Genius of the master of the house. Here simple beliefs and elementary cult acts had continued virtually unchanged from the very earliest period down to the present. These cults did not need any formal restoration on the part of the emperor, for they had not experienced the decline which the other cults had suffered, but by just so much more they would afford a firm foundation for his empire and his own rule if he could in some way succeed in connecting them with himself. In the case of Vesta this was comparatively easy. The Pontifex Maximus was the guardian of the Vestal virgins, and thus on March 6, B.C. 12, when Augustus became Pontifex Maximus, it was quite natural that there should be a festival to Vesta and that the day should continue as a public holiday. The Pontifex [Pg 177] Maximus however was supposed to live in the Regia down in the Forum, where Julius Caesar as Pontifex Maximus had actually lived. This Augustus did not desire to do, hence he gracefully gave up the Regia to the Vestal virgins and made his official residence in his own house on the Palatine, fulfilling the religious requirements by consecrating a part of that house. On a portion of the section thus consecrated a temple of Vesta was built and dedicated April 28, B.C. 12. This was strictly speaking his own "Vesta," the hearth of his own house, but the prominence of the temple of Vesta there had an effect similar to the prominence of the temple of Apollo on the Palatine, and the whole state began thus to worship at the hearth of the emperor, and in time the emperor was worshipped at each individual hearth.

But the crowning touch of Augustus's religious policy was yet to come; this was the establishment of the worship of the Genius of the emperor. After Actium and in the earlier years of his reign it is certain that Augustus would not have thought of putting himself, even in the spiritualised form of his Genius, before the people as an object of worship. But the tendency to emperor-worship which Oriental influence had brought with it was not without its effects on the emperor himself, and perhaps these effects were all the stronger because of his valiant struggle against it. Then too the state was already worshipping the gods of his family, even Vesta [Pg 178] Augusta, the goddess of his own hearth. He had become in substance, even if not yet in name, the father of his country. It had been an immemorial custom that the members of the household should worship the Genius of the master of the house. In every household in Rome that custom still existed. It was a very logical step, and one therefore which a Roman could easily take, to carry out the analogy of the family and to allow the whole state to worship the Genius of the emperor, who was the head of the family of the state. The idea therefore was not at all incongruous, nor was the way in which it was carried out, though the latter was so ingenious as to deserve special consideration.

In the old days when Rome was a farming community, the guardianship of the gods over the fields was one of the most important elements in religious life. The gods were above all the protectors of the boundary lines, and thus it came to pass that where two roads crossed and thus the corners of four farms came together the deities protecting these farms were worshipped together as the Lares Compitales, the Lares of the *compita* or cross-roads. Curiously enough this worship was later extended to the crossing of city streets, and as was natural it became more highly organised in the city than it had been in the country. Regular associations, *collegia,* were formed to look after the details of the worship, headed by the *magistri vicorum,* who were however not public officials [Pg 179] but merely the elected heads of these colleges, men mainly from the lower ranks of society. The contagion of civil and political strife affected these colleges as well as their more aristocratic parallels, higher up in the social scale, and turned them into local political clubs. The part played by these clubs in the civil struggles which occupied the last century of the republic was such that the Senate in B.C. 64 was compelled to dissolve them, though they were restored again six years later and existed until Caesar destroyed them entirely. But now Augustus was creating a new organisation for the city, dividing it into fourteen regions, each region containing a certain number of subdivisions called *vici*. The old "colleges of the cross-roads" afforded him just the sort of opportunity which he never failed to seize, that of seeming to restore a neglected republican institution, and at the same time of making it into a support of the monarchy. The colleges had antiquity in their favour, and their repeated suppression was clear proof of their power. They must be recognised and taken over by the state, their officials must be made into officials of the state, but, most important, their worship must be permeated with the imperial idea. This was where Augustus's skill showed itself. At every shrine of the cross-roads where of old the two Lares had been worshipped alone, a third image now took its place between them. This was the Genius Augusti, who thus formed henceforth an integral part of the [Pg 180] local worship of every part of the city. Under the presiding Genius Augusti the Lares themselves began to be known as the Lares Augusti and the cult grew in popularity so that it began to extend through all of Italy and even through the provinces of the empire, and wherever the Lares went, along with them went the worship of the Genius of the emperor.

Now that we have seen what Augustus did, the question arises irresistibly as to the measure of his success. There can be no question but that he was successful in obtaining the immediate object which he was seeking after. A formal religious life was unquestionably brought into being, and such strength as that life had was exerted in behalf of the empire. This is only in part true of the city but it is absolutely true of the provinces, where after all in the long run the balance of power was bound to lie. In every case the religious reform, begun in the city, spread rapidly through the rest of Italy and out into the provinces. There the negative elements, which hindered its growth in Rome itself, were absent. For the provinces the empire was all gain, and even a bad emperor was far better than none at all.

The politics of Augustus had recreated the religion which the politics of the last century of the republic had destroyed, had recreated it in as far as political considerations could. But the spirit of scepticism which had made possible the political [Pg 181] abuse of religion could not be driven out by any further application of politics. A form might be created, both the paraphernalia of temples and the hierarchy of priests whose business it was to perform certain cult acts, but there the power of enactment ceased. In the main the religious life of the people went on for good or for ill entirely independent of these things. All that was alive and real in the simple domestic cult went on down into the empire, and those who were faithful were faithful still. The cults of the Orient, against which Augustus had done all that he dared, still captured the minds of the vast majority of the people, and a Mithras or an Isis meant infinitely more than a Mars or a Vesta, even if Mars were the avenger of a Caesar, and Vesta the goddess of the living emperor's own hearth. Among the more intellectual classes the folly of the one set of gods, the darlings of the common people, was felt as keenly as the folly of the others, those who had been worshipped by the men of former days. Philosophy, which had had its share in the breakdown of faith, beginning in the days of the Punic wars, was now offering out of itself a substitute for the faith which it had taken away. It no longer contented itself with a destructive criticism which resulted in a negative view of life, but in Stoicism at least it strove to provide something sufficiently constructive to afford not only a rule of living but also an inspiration to live. [Pg 182]

With the death of Augustus the last chapter in the history of old Roman religion was closed. His was the last attempt to fill the spiritual need of the people with the old forms and the old ideas; for what he offered was in the main old though certain new ideas were mixed with it. From now on the lifeless platitudes of philosophy and the orgiastic excesses of the Oriental cults divided the field between them, and it was with them rather than with the gods of Numa or even with the deities of the Sibylline books that Christianity fought its battles. That too is a fascinating study, but it is quite another story and with the death of Augustus our present tale is told. And when we look back over the whole of it the main outlines become perhaps even clearer because of the details into which we have been compelled to go.

We see at the start the simple religion of an agricultural people still strongly tinged with animism and inheriting from an animistic past a certain formalism which is so great that it almost becomes a content. Toward the close of the kingdom we see this religion developing through Italic influences so that it takes into itself a certain number of elements which were absent from the older religion because they had no concomitants in daily life, but whose presence is now rendered necessary. These elements are especially the ideas of politics, trade, commerce, and the liberal arts. Then for a moment under [Pg 183] Servius an equilibrium seems to have been reached, and a religion to have been brought into being which was simple enough for the old lovers of simplicity and varied enough to satisfy the new demands of the community. But this was not for long, for the spiritual conquest of Rome by Greece began then, three centuries before the physical conquest of Greece by Rome. The hosts of Greek deities invaded and captured Rome under the leadership of the Sibylline books, and though at first they had been kept outside the *pomerium,* even this iron barrier was melted in the heat of the Second Punic War, and the new Greek gods swarmed into the city proper. At the same time as a last heritage from the baleful books an Oriental goddess, the Magna Mater, was taken into the cult and into the hearts of the people, and the elements of decay were thus all present. These elements were threefold: the natural spiritual reaction resulting from the excesses of the period of the Second Punic War; the fascination of the Orient, exhibited to Rome in the cult of the Magna Mater; and the new gift which Greece now made to Rome, the knowledge of her literature, especially of her philosophy. In the last two centuries of the republic then these forces alone would have been sufficient to cause the downfall of religion, but they were aided by politics, which fastened itself upon the formalism of the state religion and sucked the little life-blood that was left. Rome's scholars and wise men could deplore [Pg 184] the result and point out the causes, but they could not cure the state of affairs. What politics had done, politics alone could undo, hence only the reforms of an autocrat could restore something of the outward structure of the old state religion. But beyond this politics and the autocrat were alike powerless. Against philosophy and Oriental ecstasy they were of no avail. Hence the spirit had left the religion which Augustus had restored even before the marble temples which he had built in its honour had fallen into decay.

The age of formalism had passed, the religious demands of the individual could no longer be satisfied by a mere ritual. For good or for evil something more personal, more subjective, was needed. Men sought for it in various ways and with varying success, but except in the simple forms of family worship old Roman religion was dead.

THE END.

HANDBOOKS OF

ARCHÆOLOGY & ANTIQUITIES

EDITED BY

Professor Percy Gardner, Litt. D. of the University of Oxford, and Professor Francis W. Kelsey, of the University of Michigan.

Extra Crown 8vo.

GREEK SCULPTURE. By Prof. Ernest A. Gardner, M.A. Second Impression, with Appendix. Part I., 5s. Part II., 5s. Complete in one vol. 10s.

Appendix separate, 1s. net.

GREEK AND ROMAN COINS. By G.F. Hill, of the Coins Department of the British Museum. Illustrated. 9s.

THE ROMAN FESTIVALS OF THE PERIOD OF THE REPUBLIC. By W. Warde Fowler, M.A. 6s.

A HANDBOOK OF GREEK CONSTITUTIONAL HISTORY. By A.H.J. Greenidge, M.A. With Map. 5s.

THE DESTRUCTION OF ANCIENT ROME. A Sketch of the History of the Monuments. By Rodolfo Lanciani. 6s.

ROMAN PUBLIC LIFE. By A.H.J. Greenidge, M.A. 10s. 6d.

CHRISTIAN ART AND ARCHÆOLOGY. A Handbook to the Monuments of the Early Church. By W. Lowrie, M.A. 10s. 6d.

GRAMMAR OF GREEK ART. By Professor Percy Gardner, Litt. D. Illustrated. 7s. 6d.

MACMILLAN AND CO.'S PUBLICATIONS

ANNUAL OF THE BRITISH SCHOOL AT ATHENS. Crown 4to. No. I. Session 1894-1895, 35. 6d. net.; No. III. Session 1896-1897, 10s. 6d. net; No. IV. Session 1897-1898, 7s. 6d. net; No. V. Session 1898-

1899, 7s. 6d. net; No. VI. Session 1896-1900, 10s. 6d. net; No. VII. Session 1900-1901, 12s. 6d. net; No. VIII. Session 1901-1902, 17s. net.; No. IX. Session 1902-1903, 21s. net.; No. X. Session 1903-1904, 17s. net.

HELLENIC SOCIETY'S PUBLICATIONS

EXCAVATIONS AT MEGALOPOLIS, 1890-1891. By E.A. Gardner, W. Loring, G.C. Richards, and W.J. Woodhouse. With an architectural description by R.W. Schultz. 4to. 25s. net.

ECCLESIASTICAL SITES IN ISAURIA (CILICIA TRACHEA). By the Rev. A.C. Headlam. Imperial 4to. 5s. net.

PLANS AND DRAWINGS OF ATHENIAN BUILDINGS. By Professor J.H. Middleton, Litt. D. Edited by Professor E.A. Gardner. 8vo. 7s. 6d. net.

EXCAVATIONS AT PHYLAKOPI IN MELOS. By T.D. Atkinson, A.C. Bosanquet, C.C. Edgar, A.J. Evans, D.G. Hogarth, D. Mackenzie, C. Smith, and F.B. Welch. Imperial 8vo. 30s. net.

JOURNAL OF HELLENIC STUDIES. 8vo. Vols. 30s. net.; Parts, 15s. net.

CATALOGUE OF BOOKS IN THE LIBRARY OF THE SOCIETY. Imperial 8vo. 3s. net.

PAPERS OF THE BRITISH SCHOOL AT ROME. Super-Royal 8vo. Vol. I. 25s. net; Vol. II. Sixteenth Century Drawings of Roman Buildings. Crown 4to. 30s. net. In Special Binding, 35s. net.

Works by Professor RODOLFO LANCIANI, LL. D.,

Professor of Archæology in the University of Rome.

THE RUINS AND EXCAVATIONS OF ANCIENT ROME. A Companion for Students and Travellers. Illustrated. Crown 8vo, [*New edition in preparation.*

ANCIENT ROME IN THE LIGHT OF RECENT DISCOVERIES. 4to. 24s.

PAGAN AND CHRISTIAN ROME. 4to. 24s.

NEW TALES OF OLD ROME. Illustrated. 4to. 24s.

MACMILLAN AND CO., Ltd., LONDON.